VOGUE KNITTING

BEGINNER BASICS

VOGUE® KNITTING
BEGINNER
BASICS

SIXTH&SPRING BOOKS
NEW YORK

SIXTH&SPRING BOOKS

233 Spring Street
New York, New York 10013

Library of Congress Cataloging-in-Publication Data

Vogue knitting beginner basics / [book editor, Trisha Malcolm].--1st ed.
     p. cm. -- (Vogue knitting on the go!)
     ISBN 1-931543-31-3
     1. Knitting. 2. Knitting--Patterns. I. Title: Beginner basics. II. Malcolm, Trisha, 1960-
III. Vogue knitting international. IV. Series.

   TT820 .V6243 2003
   746.43--dc21   2002044560

Manufactured in China

1 3 5 7 9 10 8 6 4 2

First Edition

INTRODUCTION

Welcome to the wonderful world of knitting! By picking up a pair of needles and a ball of yarn, you embark on the exciting journey of learning a new craft; one that has the potential to bring you joy for many years to come. Knitting brings out your creative side, offers you a sense of accomplishment and even soothes your nerves at the end of a long day. It's portable, versatile and full of endless possibilities. In every way, shape and form, knitting is a great skill to learn.

One of the best ways to learn to knit is to master one skill at a time, working your way up to more challenging projects as time goes on. This book takes you step-by-step through this process, incorporating new techniques and tips into scarves, hats, sweaters and accessories that are as fun to make as they are to wear.

In this busy world of ours, few people have the time to sit down for one long stretch to learn something new. The learning must occur in spurts, slipped in between the many events that shape your everyday. With their small size and approachable projects, *Knitting on the Go* books are designed to fit perfectly into such found moments. Take your needles and yarn along on a business trip, to the movies or even to a family gathering. You'll be well on your way to being a master knitter in no time.

So, turn the page and let's get started. It's time to learn to KNIT ON THE GO!

EASY DOES IT

GETTING STARTED

Are you ready to knit? Whether you've always wanted to learn how, or have just recently begun to yearn for the sound of needles clicking together, welcome! You've picked a great place to start.

The three sections of this book are designed with the new knitter in mind. In the first section we'll take you step by step through the process of learning to knit: from the very basics of making your first stitch to later on when we'll explore the ins-and-outs of decreasing, increasing, seaming and other essential techniques.

Once you feel confident with the basics of knitting, move on to the second section where you'll find numerous chances to practice. From a fabulous simple scarf that involves only knit stitches to your first sweater and a sampler baby blanket, this section moves sequentially through more challenging projects to introduce new skills while giving you a chance to solidify the ones you have already mastered.

All knitters make mistakes, and so our third section is devoted to correcting all of those little errors that tend to crop up. Learn how to fix a twisted stitch, pick up a knit or purl that has escaped from the needle and even remedy an incomplete stitch.

You've chosen a truly wonderful craft to learn, and we're sure you're eager to begin. So, gather up some basic supplies, get comfortable and let's get started.

■ NEEDLES

Though knitting needles share a name with their sharper sisters, they really should not be sharp at all. Needles come in many different styles and lengths and can be made out of metal, plastic, casein, bamboo and wood or more exotic materials such as ebony, rosewood, birch and walnut. Each is some variation on the "pointed stick" concept. Which to use depends on your project and personal preference, so experiment with a few different types until you find the one that suits your knitting style.

Straight needles, the ones that actually look like two individual "sticks," have been around since the beginning of time, and are the tools most of us associate with knitting. Sold in pairs in varying lengths (the most common being 10 and 14 inches), they sport a point on one end and a knob at the other that keeps stitches from sliding off as you knit.

Circular needles appeared on the scene in the early part of the 20th century, an event heralded by some as the best thing ever to happen to knitting. Made up of shorter pointed "sticks" attached to one another by a smooth nylon cord, circular needles can be used to knit both tubular and flat pieces and are ideal for knitting in tight spaces (e.g. crowded buses, subways, movie theaters). They've also solved the problem of the missing needle; you'll never lose one in the couch cushions or have it roll away from you during a plane's descent.

KNITTING NEEDLES

U.S.	Metric	U.S.	Metric	U.S.	Metric
0	2.00mm	7	4.50mm	15	10.00mm
1	2.25mm	8	5.00mm	17	12.75mm
2	2.75mm	9	5.50mm	19	15.00mm
3	3.25mm	10	6.00mm	35	19.00mm
4	3.50mm	10.5	6.50mm	50	25.50mm
5	3.75mm	11	8.00mm		
6	4.00mm	13	9.00mm		

CROCHET HOOKS

U.S.	Metric	U.S.	Metric	U.S.	Metric
14 steel	.60mm	C/2	2.75mm	I/9	5.50mm
12 steel	.75mm	D/3	3.25mm	J/10	6.00mm
10 steel	1.00mm	E/4	3.50mm	K/10.5	6.50mm
6 steel	1.50mm	F/5	3.75mm	L/11	8.00mm
5 steel	1.75mm	G/6	4.00mm	M/13	9.00mm
B/1	2.25mm	H/8	5.00mm	N/15	10.00mm

The third and final variation on knitting needles are the double-pointed style (dpn). These have points on both ends and are used to knit small items in the round, turn sock heels and the like. They're a bit trickier to use than straights and circulars, so most knitters wait until later in their knitting careers to use them.

All needles—straight, circular or double pointed—come in a wide range of standardized sizes. They are marked in numeric U.S. sizes (0-50) or millimeters (2.00-25.50) which indicate the diameter of the needle. As a general rule, the lower the number, the thin-ner the needle. See the chart above for a full listing of sizes. Note: We've also given you a crochet hook chart for future reference.

■ YARN

Now we get to the fun part—yarn, and lots of it. Take your pick from natural fibers like wool, alpaca, angora, cashmere, cotton, linen, silk and mohair or sleek synthetics that range from inexpensive acrylic to pricey, glitzy rayon novelties and even new age materials like microfiber and paper. Thick, thin, smooth or textured, you'll find them in solid colors as well as striped, variegated (lengths of different colors alternated within the same ball) and multicolored patterns. Make a trip to your local knitting store and take a good look at the multitude of choices available. Chances are you'll never have time to try them all!

Whether spun from wool or paper, traditional or cutting edge, all yarn is grouped into basic categories to help you choose the right type for your project. Organized by weight (thickness of the yarn) they range from super fine all the way to super bulky.

Okay, so now you're on your way to grasping the basics of yarn and needle size. But how do they work together? With rare exceptions (like some kinds of lace knitting), thinner yarns work best on thinner needles, while thicker yarns require a needle with a little more heft. We'll discuss gauge and needle size later in the book, but for now you just need to know that each yarn weight has a corresponding range of recommended needle sizes. The chart on the next page will help you familiarize yourself with how it all fits together.

▦ HOLDING YOUR YARN AND NEEDLES TOGETHER

One of the biggest frustrations for a new knitter is finding the most comfortable way of holding the yarn and needles, so if you're reading this and thinking you'll never figure it out, don't despair. With just a little time and patience your hands will fall into a comfortable rhythm.

Perhaps what makes learning to hold the yarn and needles a bit confusing is that no two people do it the same way. The two main styles of knitting are the English and the Continental. Though both create the same end product, most knitters have very specific opinions about which way is superior (their way, of course!). If someone has already taught you how to knit, chances are you have inadvertently chosen one way over the other. If not, or if you'd like to see how the other side knits, here's the major difference: English knitters hold and "throw" the yarn with their right hand, while Continental knitters manipulate the yarn with their left hand.

Once you've decided which hand will hold the working yarn, there's still one more decision to make—how to hold the needles. Some knitters like to grasp their needles over the top, while others would rather hold them like pencils, resting the majority of the needle between the thumb and index finger. There is honestly no right or wrong way to accomplish this, so experiment with the different choices and pretty soon you will have developed your own unique style.

TIP

Don't toss away that little piece of paper wrapped around the yarn. Officially known as a "ball band," this handy label contains essential information about fiber content, color, dye lot, yardage/meters and grams, suggested needle size/gauge and care instructions.

Categories of yarn, gauge ranges and recommended needle and hook sizes

Yarn Weight Symbol & Category Names	1 Super Fine	2 Fine	3 Light	4 Medium	5 Bulky	6 Super Bulky
Type of Yarns in Category	Sock, Fingering, Baby	Sport, Baby	DK, Light Worsted	Worsted, Afghan, Aran	Chunky, Craft, Rug	Super Bulky, Roving
Knit Gauge Range* in Stockinette Stitch to 4 inches	27–32 sts	23–26 sts	21–24 sts	16–20 sts	12–15 sts	6–11 sts
Recommended Needle in Metric Size Range	2.25–3.25 mm	3.25–3.75 mm	3.75–4.5 mm	4.5–5.5 mm	5.5–8 mm	9–15 mm and larger
Recommended Needle U.S. size range	1 to 3	3 to 5	5 to 7	7 to 9	9 to 11	11 to 19 and larger
Crochet Gauge* Ranges in Single Crochet to 4 inch	21–32 sts	16–20 sts	12–17 sts	11–14 sts	8–11 sts	5–9 sts
Recommended Hook in Metric Size Range	2.25–3.5 mm	3.5–4.5 mm	4.5–5.5 mm	5.5–6.5 mm	6.5–9 mm	9–12 mm and larger
Recommended Hook U.S. Size Range	B-1 to E-4	E-4 to 7	7 to I-9	I-9 to K-10½	K-10½ to M-13	M-13 to P-16 and larger

FIRST STITCHES

You've purchased your yarn and needles and figured out (at least tentatively) how to hold them all together. Now it's time to get started! But just one more thing—isn't there always one more thing—before you can start knitting to your heart's content, you need to make the foundation row that will set the stage for all the stitches to follow. You need to cast on.

▪ SLIP KNOT

This is the stitch to start all stitches; the one that anchors the yarn to the needles and makes it possible to cast on. Before starting the slip knot, decide which method of casting on you want to try. If you choose the double cast-on method, leave approximately an inch for every stitch that you're about to place on the needle. For the knit-on cast-on, leave eight to ten inches between the end of the yarn and the slip knot.

▪ CASTING ON

Although there are numerous ways to get those first stitches on the needle, we have chosen two of the most basic, sturdy and neat-looking versions to get you started. The first technique, a double cast-on, uses one needle and two lengths of yarn, while the knit-on variation uses two needles and one strand of yarn. If you like one of these methods better than the other, go with it! Remember, this is for fun and relaxation, and you pretty much can't do it wrong. How many other parts of your life can you say that about?

A firm cast-on row makes for a good project to come. Practice casting on with your favorite technique until it feels like second nature and the stitches appear uniform in size and spacing.

SLIP KNOT

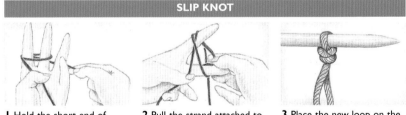

I Hold the short end of the yarn in your palm with your thumb. Wrap the yarn twice around the index and middle fingers.

2 Pull the strand attached to the ball through the loop between your two fingers, forming a new loop.

3 Place the new loop on the needle. Tighten the loop on the needle by pulling on both ends of the yarn to form the slip knot. You are now ready to begin one of the following cast-on methods.

Here's a piece of advice: when you first learn to cast on, your foundation row may be so tight that it's difficult to get your needle into the little loops, much less wrap the yarn around and come out with something that resembles a stitch. If that happens, try casting on with two needles held together or with a needle two sizes larger than you'll be using for the rest of the project. If, on the other hand, you find yourself with a beginning edge that looks like it was made with a toilet paper roll, try casting on to a needle two sizes smaller, and the situation should improve.

DOUBLE CAST-ON

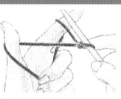  

I Make a slip knot on the right needle, leaving a long tail. Wind the tail end around your left thumb, front to back. Wrap the yarn from the ball over your left index finger and secure the ends in your palm.

2 Insert the needle upward in the loop on your thumb. Then with the needle, draw the yarn from the ball through the loop to form a stitch.

3 Take your thumb out of the loop and tighten the loop on the needle. Continue in this way until all the stitches are cast on.

KNIT-ON CAST-ON

I Make a slip knot on the left needle. *Insert the right needle knitwise into the stitch on the left needle. Wrap the yarn around the right needle as if to knit.

2 Draw the yarn through the first stitch to make a new stitch, but do not drop the stitch from the left needle.

3 Slip the new stitch to the left needle as shown. Repeat from the * until the required number of stitches is cast on.

AND YOU'RE OFF!

▨ KNIT STITCH

Finally, the moment you've been waiting for. Your cast on is picture perfect (or almost), and now it's time to knit. Like we said before, there are two different ways to make each knit stitch (English or Continental method), and the one you choose depends largely on which you're most comfortable with.

It may take awhile to feel comfortable with this new motion, but keep practicing and you'll get it. It may help to have a seasoned knitter help you learn the ropes.

▨ GARTER STITCH

This is the most basic of all stitch patterns, and is achieved by knitting every row. The

KNIT STITCH ENGLISH

I Hold the needle with the cast-on stitches in your left hand. Hold the working needle in your right hand, wrapping the yarn around your fingers.

2 Insert the right needle from front to back into the first cast-on stitch on the left needle. Keep the right needle under the left needle and the yarn at the back.

3 Wrap the yarn under and over the right needle in a clockwise motion.

4 With the right needle, catch the yarn and pull it through the cast-on stitch.

5 Slip the cast-on stitch off the left needle, leaving the newly formed stitch on the right needle. Repeat these steps in each subsequent stitch until all stitches have been worked from the left needle. You have made one row of knit stitches.

end result is a flat, reversible, ridged fabric that stands up well to wear and does not roll at the edges.

Here's how to do it: When you get to the end of your first row of knit stitches, transfer the full needle to your left hand and start the process of knitting each stitch all over again. After several rows you'll begin to see the fruits of your labor (a very rewarding moment indeed), and in time your growing strip of garter stitch will start to look like a real piece of knitted fabric.

KNIT STITCH CONTINENTAL

1 Hold the needles in the same way as the English method on page 16, but hold the yarn with your left hand rather than your right.

2 Insert the right needle from front to back into the first cast-on stitch on the left needle. Keep the right needle under the left needle, with the yarn in back of both needles.

3 Lay the yarn over the right needle as shown.

4 With the tip of the right needle, pull the strand through the cast-on stitch, holding the strand with the right index finger if necessary.

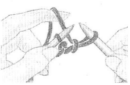

5 Slip the cast-on stitch off the left needle, leaving the newly formed stitch on the right needle. Continue to repeat these steps until you have worked all of the stitches from the left needle to the right needle. You have made one row of knit stitches.

GARTER STITCH

Cast on any number of stitches. Knit every row.

■ PURL STITCH

Take a deep breath and stretch your fingers, because it's time to learn the second all-important stitch in the world of knitting: the purl stitch.

Purling is basically just a backwards version of knitting, and when you put the two together you can come up with literally hundreds of stitch patterns. Some people find the purl stitch to be a bit more awkward to work than the knit stitch (which is why we teach the knit stitch first). If you don't get it at first, just keep trying. Much like learning to ride a bicycle, once you understand how to purl, it will feel like old hat.

PURL STITCH ENGLISH

I As with the knit stitch, hold the working needle in your right hand and the needle with the stitches in your left. The yarn is held and manipulated with your right hand and is kept to the front of the work.

2 Insert the right needle from back to front into the first stitch on the left needle. The right needle is now in front of the left needle and the yarn is at the front of the work.

3 With your right index finger, wrap the yarn counterclockwise around the right needle.

4 Draw the right needle and the yarn backward through the stitch on the left needle, forming a loop on the right needle.

5 Slip the stitch off the left needle. You have made one purl stitch. Repeat these steps in each subsequent stitch until all stitches have been worked from the left needle. You have made one row of purl stitches.

STOCKINETTE STITCH

Now that you've learned how to knit and purl, you can finally put them together to make stockinette stitch, the V-patterned fabric that people most often associate with knitting. Unlike garter stitch (which appears ridged and does not roll), stockinette stitch has a much smoother appearance and a tendency to curl at the edges. Many designers use this inclination to their advantage, creating everything from rolled necks and cuffs to rolled edges of handbags and scarves.

1 As with the knit stitch, hold the working needle in your right hand and the needle with the stitches in your left. The yarn is held and manipulated with your left hand and is kept to the front of the work.

2 Insert the right needle from back to front into the first stitch on the left needle, keeping the yarn in front of the work.

3 Lay the yarn over the right needle as shown. Pull down on the yarn with your left index finger to keep the yarn taut.

4 Bring the right needle and the yarn backward through the stitch on the left needle, forming a loop on the right needle.

5 Slide the stitch off the left needle. Use your left index finger to tighten the new purl stitch on the right needle. Continue to repeat these steps until you have worked all of the stitches from the left needle to the right needle. You have made one row of purl stitches.

Cast on any number of stitches.
Row 1 (right side) Knit.
Row 2 Purl.
Repeat rows 1 and 2.

■ BASIC RIBBING

Alternating entire rows of knit and purl stitches creates the well-known stockinette stitch, but it's also possible to switch back and forth within the same row to produce numerous different patterns.

Of all the knit/purl stitch patterns you will learn, ribbing is definitely the most widely used. Because of its stretchiness and ability to "bounce" back into place, ribbing makes up the hems, necks and cuffs of most sweaters. Many sweaters even use ribbing throughout the garment to create a slim, body-hugging effect.

One of the nice things about ribbing (besides its elasticity) is that after the first row or two you can put down the instructions and let the stitches show you what comes

next. When the stitch you're about to work looks like a V, knit it. When it looks like a bump, purl it.

The trickiest part about ribbing for beginners is remembering to move the yarn back and forth when working the different stitches. For example, in two-by-two ribbing, you knit two stitches, move the yarn between the two needles to the front of the work and then purl two stitches. When you are ready to knit again, return the yarn to the back of the work by passing it between the two needles, then continue with your pattern. If you don't move the yarn from back to front and front to back between knit and purl stitches, you will end up with extra stitches on your needle and a rectangular piece that quickly begins to resemble a triangle.

MOVING YARN BACK AND FORTH

When knitting a stitch, the yarn is always held at the back of the work. When purling a stitch, the yarn is always at the front. In ribbing, when you change from a knit to a purl stitch, you must be sure the yarn is in the correct position to work the next stitch. When you are moving the yarn from the back to the front, or vice versa, the yarn should go between the two needles, and not over them.

knitwise

purlwise

TIE ONE ON

■ JOINING YARN

At some point you'll be knitting along, feeling confident and picking up speed, when all of a sudden—poof!—you've run out of yarn. Don't panic—there's a very easy way to remedy that situation, and it's called "joining yarn."

Whenever possible, join new yarn at the end of a row, even if that means cutting off some of the yarn from the previous ball. You'll find it easier to hide the ends later, and stitches will be less likely to bulge or become distorted mid-row. If joining mid-row can't be avoided, carefully check the tension of the affected stitch so that it's neither too tight nor too loose.

JOINING YARN

To join a new yarn at the side edge, tie it loosely around the old yarn, leaving at least a 6"/15cm tail. Untie the knot later and weave the ends into the seam (see page 24 for a description of weaving in ends).

I To join a yarn in the middle of the row, insert the right needle into the next stitch to be worked, wrap the new yarn around the right needle and start knitting with the new yarn.

2 Work to the end of the row. Tie the old and new strands together loosely before continuing so they will not unravel.

▓ DECREASING

There are a myriad of projects you can make in rectangular form, but at some point you may want to move on to items that are a bit more shaped. Decreasing (or reducing the number of stitches in a row) is one way to achieve that shaping.

There are numerous methods of decreasing that produce different looks and effects, but we are going to introduce you to a pair of the easiest and most common decreases to start: the knit two together (or k2tog) and purl two together (or p2tog) decreases. If you need to decrease two stitches at once, try SK2P (slip one stitch, knit two together, pass the slipped stitch over the knit two together) or the K3tog (knit three together).

KNIT OR PURL TWO TOGETHER DECREASE

This basic decrease slants to the right on the knit side of the work. It is abbreviated as k2tog (or p2tog).

K2TOG Insert the right needle from front to back (knitwise) into the next two stitches on the left needle. Wrap the yarn around the right needle (as when knitting) and pull it through. You have decreased one stitch.

P2TOG Insert the right needle into the front loops (purlwise) of the next two stitches on the left needle. Wrap the yarn around the right needle (as when purling) and pull it through. You have decreased one stitch.

SK2P

1 Slip the next stitch knitwise, then knit the next two stitches together as shown to decrease one stitch.

2 Pass the slipped stitch over the decreased stitch. You have decreased two stitches.

▨ INCREASING

Another way to change the number of stitches on the needle is to increase. Like with decreasing, there are several kinds of increasing; some are visible, and others blend completely into their surroundings. One of the most common variations is the bar increase, which is made by working in the front and back loops of the same stitch. It leaves a small, slightly visible bar (thus the name) on the right side of the work. This bar can either be hidden in a seam or used as decoration.

BAR INCREASE

1 To increase on the knit side, insert the right needle knitwise into the stitch to be increased. Wrap the yarn around the right needle and pull it through as if knitting, but leave the stitch on the left needle.

2 Insert the right needle into the back of the same stitch. Wrap the yarn around the needle and pull it through. Slip the stitch from the left needle. You now have two stitches on the right needle.

WORKING IN FRONT AND BACK LOOPS

The front of the stitch is the loop closest to you, and the loop that you'll normally work into. To knit into the front loop, insert the right needle from left to right into the stitch on the left needle. To knit into the back loop (loop farthest from you), insert right needle from right to left under left needle and into stitch. To purl into the front loop, insert needle from right to left into stitch. To purl into the back loop, insert needle from behind into stitch.

Knitting into the front loop

Purling into the front loop

Knitting into the back loop

Purling into the back loop

FINISHING FIRST

■ BASIC KNIT BIND-OFF

Once your knitted fabric is as long as you want it to be, you'll need to bind off its top stitches in order to prevent it from unraveling into an unfortunate pile of yarn on the floor. Binding off is generally a very easy process, with only one thing to watch out for: tension. Knitters often bind off too tightly, creating a pucker at the top of all that hard work. To avoid this, try binding off with a needle two sizes larger than you were using for the project.

We have shown the basic knit bind-off over stockinette stitch, but the process is exactly the same when binding off garter stitch.

■ WEAVING IN ENDS

Every time you finish a ball of yarn and join a new one or change colors in the middle of a stripe pattern, you'll find yourself with loose ends. In order to tuck in these stragglers and create a truly finished looking product, you must weave them into the wrong side of the knitted fabric.

To do this, carefully untie the knot you made when joining new yarn. Thread one of the loose strands through a yarn needle (see Extra, Extra! on pages 44-48) and snake the needle (and attached yarn) down through approximately five of the free loops along the edge of your knitting. Snip close to the work to remove whatever's left, being very careful not to cut into the actual knitting. To secure the second strand, thread it through the yarn needle and weave up.

If you have to change yarns in the middle of a row, untie the knot and weave one loose piece in each horizontal direction, following the path of the affected stitch through five or six additional stitches on the wrong side of the work. Always double check the right side of the fabric to make sure there is no puckering or unsightly looseness where the ends began.

1 Knit two stitches. *Insert the left needle into the first stitch on the right needle.

2 Pull this stitch over the second stitch and off the right needle.

3 One stitch remains on the right needle as shown. Knit the next stitch. Repeat from the * until you have bound off the required number of stitches.

At first glance, knitting instructions can look intimidating. They seem to be written in a completely different language from the one you're used to, and contain all sorts of new concepts and abbreviations that you're not familiar with. Follow along as we help you decipher the knitter's code.

■ GAUGE

The first step in garment making, and possibly the most important step of all, is making the gauge swatch. The gauge swatch is basically just a square piece of knitted fabric that demonstrates how you, the needles and the yarn interact before you get going on the main project. All patterns give a recommended gauge, or stitches and rows per inch, at the beginning of their instructions, usually directly below the suggestions for yarn weight and needle size.

In order to make the gauge swatch, gather up the exact yarn and needles that you plan to use for your project (even small differences like yarn color and needle brand can affect your gauge!). Cast on a number of stitches that will give you at least four inches across, and then work in stockinette stitch or the specified stitch pattern until

GAUGE

See the importance of making a gauge swatch with these two squares of knitting. Each is made with the same exact number of stitches and rows, but the one on the left uses a needle one size smaller than the one on the right. Does it inspire you to make a gauge swatch before starting a whole garment? We hope so!

You can measure your gauge swatch between selvage stitches using a tape measure, as the first two photos show. Or you can use a stitch gauge in the center of your swatch and count the stitches and rows inside the two-inch (5cm) right angle opening, as shown in the third photo.

you have made a bit more than four vertical inches of fabric.

At this point, simply remove the needle from the stitches (without binding off) and place the sample on a flat, smooth surface like a hardwood floor or kitchen table. Using a tape measure, ruler or stitch gauge, measure across four inches of the knitting in both directions and count the number of stitches within those four inches (don't forget fractions of stitches). If you have more stitches to the inch than the pattern recommends, go up one needle size. If you have fewer stitches than is desirable, try again with a smaller needle.

Once you get as close as possible to the recommended gauge, go ahead and start knitting your garment, but don't forget about gauge altogether just yet. (You thought you were done with the gauge thing, didn't you?)

TIP

Make your gauge swatch easier to work with by including selvage stitches on the edges of the square. These help the piece of fabric lay nice and flat, and also simplify the process of measuring by giving you definite edges between which to measure. To make selvage stitches, work two rows of garter stitch (knit every row) at the top and bottom of the swatch and include two stitches on the beginning and end of each stockinette row that are garter stitch as well.

Sometimes the gauge of your swatch may differ from the gauge that results when you cast on all of the stitches required for your garment. After you've worked about 5"/12 cm of the first piece of your project, recheck your gauge by laying the piece down on a flat surface and pulling out your tape measure (or stitch gauge) again. Your knitting should be just as close to the recommended gauge as it was before, but in the event that it's not, you'll have to unravel what you've done and start again using a different needle size. As you rip out the rows and roll the yarn back into a ball, know two things: one, that you'll be glad you did when your sweater fits, and two, that you have our condolences.

TIP

Most knitters mistakenly think that making the gauge swatch is an extra, unnecessary step that can be avoided altogether. If there's one piece of advice we hope you'll remember, it's this: always, always, always make a gauge swatch! If your knitting is so much as a half of an inch off from the recommended gauge you can end up with a HUGE difference in the size of your finished garment. Take it from us that there's nothing quite as frustrating as working tirelessly on an adult's hat that ends up being the size of a toddler's, or making a baby's hat that would fit best on a gorilla.

Once you start working with knitting patterns, you'll notice that they seem to be written in a completely different language. What, after all, does "*K1, p1; rep from *" mean? All of these seemingly cryptic strings of letters, numbers and symbols are part of a system of knitting terminology that help save space in patterns and make instructions less tedious to read. Here we list and describe the terms you'll run across in this book.

approx: approximately

beg: begin, beginning

cont: continue

dec: decrease

in/cm/mm: inches/centimeters/millimeters

inc: increase

inc (dec)...sts evenly across row: Count the number of stitches in the row, and then divide that number by the number of stitches to be increased (decreased). The result of this division will tell you how many stitches to work between each increased (decreased) stitch.

k the knit and p the purl sts: This is a phrase used when a pattern of knit and purl stitches has been established and will be continued for some time. When the stitch that's facing you looks like a V, knit it. When it looks like a bump, purl it.

k: knit

k2tog: knit two together (a method of decreasing explained on page 22)

k3tog: knit three together Worked same as k2tog, but insert needle into 3 sts instead of 2 for a double decrease.

knitwise: Insert the needle into the stitch as if you were going to knit it.

oz/g: ounces/grams (usually in reference to amount of yarn in a single ball)

p: purl

p2tog: purl two together (a method of decreasing explained on page 22)

pat: pattern

purlwise: Insert the needle into the stitch as if you were going to purl it.

SK2P: Slip one, knit two together, pass slipped stitch over k2tog (explained on page 22).

rem: remain, remains or remaining

rep: repeat

rep from *: Repeat the instructions after the asterisk as many times as indicated. If the directions say "rep from * to end," continue to repeat the instructions after the asterisk to the end of the row.

rev sc: reverse single crochet

reverse shaping: A term used for garments such as cardigans where shaping for the right and left fronts is identical, but reversed. For example, neck edge stitches that were decreased at the beginning of the row for the first piece will be decreased

at the end of the row on the second. In general, follow the directions for the first piece, being sure to mirror the decreases (increases) on each side.

RS: right side

sc: single crochet

SKP: Slip one stitch knitwise to right-hand needle. Knit the next stitch and pass the slipped stitch over the knit stitch.

slip: Transfer the indicated stitches from the left to the right needle without working (knitting or purling) them.

Small (Medium, Large): The most common method of displaying changes in pattern for different sizes. In general, the measurements, stitch counts, directions, etc. for the smallest size come first, followed by the increasingly larger sizes in parentheses. If there is only one number given, it applies to all of the sizes.

st/sts: stitch/stitches

St st: stockinette stitch

work even: Continue in the established pattern without working any increases or decreases.

WS: wrong side

yo: yarn over

■ UNDERSTANDING SCHEMATICS

Towards the end of every sweater pattern there are line drawings, with bullets and numbers skirting the sides and words like "Back" and "Left Front" scrawled across the centers. These are called schematics, and have some important uses in the world of sweater making.

First and foremost, schematics, which are drawn to scale, give you an at-a-glance run-down of all the measurements, angles and shapes of the sweater you're about to make. They tell you if the sweater tapers at the waist or narrows at the shoulders, as well as indicating the exact depth and width of the armholes, bust and sleeves. The most exciting part about schematics is that they give you a mini-representation of what your sweater pieces will look like when you've finished knitting them.

In general, the simpler the sweater, the simpler the schematic. The basic drawings to the right are good examples of schematics for a beginner-level woman's pullover sweater. The numbers outside the parentheses represent the smallest size, while the numbers inside the parentheses indicate measurements for sequentially increasing sizes.

The schematics for a cardigan are much like those for a pullover sweater, but with one main difference: the fronts. In general, one of the two fronts will be drawn, and then you just have to imagine (or sketch) a mirror image for the other. Not so hard, right?

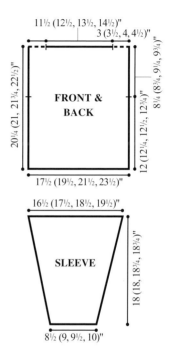

DECONSTRUCTING
SWEATER CONSTRUCTION

When you've finished knitting the pieces for a sweater, it's time to put them together. We recommend blocking (see page 32) before assembly. The general sequence of sweater assembly proceeds as follows: First, connect the shoulders. Second, finish the neck edge (with a neckband, hemming, etc.). Third, sew the sleeves to the body of the sweater. And finally, sew continuously from the end of the sleeve to the underarm, and then down the body of the sweater to the bottom edge. This all sounds straightforward enough, but allow us to give you some tips that will make the final construction as easy and professional-looking as possible.

■ MARKING FOR ARMHOLES

With dropped shoulders (the simplest sweater shape and construction), it's especially important to secure the sleeves in the same place on both sides of the body so that the top seams rest squarely on the center of the shoulder. One fail-safe way to make sure this happens is to mark the front and back pieces for the armhole as you knit. To do this, determine the width of the top of the sleeve (also called the upper arm) using the schematic. Divide this number in half to know how much of the sleeve will reside on each side of the body. Subtract half of the upper arm width from the total length of the body, and then mark the body pieces on each side when you've knit to that length.

Got all that? If not, here's an example: Let's say that the upper width of each sleeve is 16", and that the total body length is 22". Divide 16" by 2 to get 8" on each side of the body. 22-8 = 14", the length from the bottom edge of the sweater to the beginning of the armhole. Periodically measure the body as you knit, and when you reach 14", place a marker (either a safety pin or a stitch marker) on each end of your knitted piece. Finish knitting the body as instructed in the pattern. Repeat this same process for the other body piece, and when you go to attach the sleeves, it will be a breeze.

■ KNITTING SHOULDERS
TOGETHER

Although you can always simply bind off the shoulders and sew them together, you can also use this clever device for constructing shoulder seams: the three-needle bind-off. This trick streamlines two processes of finishing (binding off and seaming) into one, and has the added bonus of creating a join that is simultaneously very strong and not bulky.

To knit the shoulders together, you will need three needles: one holding each of the two shoulder tops, and one with which you complete the bind off. If you don't have three needles of the same size, that's okay. You can use smaller needles to hold the shoulder stitches as long as you use the correct needle size to bind off.

To use this technique, either start with the two right sides of the sweater facing together, or begin with the wrong sides together. Starting with the right sides together creates a smooth, virtually invisible surface at the top of the shoulder, while the opposite creates a firm ridge that can be purposefully worked for decoration.

■ COUNTING ROWS

When making a sweater, it's especially important to make sure the edges match exactly before sewing them together. A hat or other simple accesory may look charming with a little variation in shape, but a sweater will probably just appear lopsided and ridiculous.

The easiest way to guarantee that your seams line up with a sweater is to take special care that both front and back pieces are exactly the same length. You have two choices about how to handle this: you can either measure the pieces as carefully as possible, or you can utilize row counters or pencil and paper to document each knitted row and thereby ensure the exact same number on each. Both choices are equally valid, and which you settle on will mostly be a matter of personal preference.

THREE-NEEDLE BIND-OFF

This bind-off is used to join two edges that have the same number of stitches, such as shoulder edges, which have been placed on holders.

1 With the right side of the two pieces facing each other, and the needles parallel, insert a third needle knitwise into the first stitch of each needle. Wrap the yarn around the needle as if to knit.

2 Knit these two stitches together and slip them off the needles. *Knit the next two stitches together in the same way as shown.

3 Slip the first stitch on the third needle over the second stitch and off the needle. Repeat from the * in step 2 across the row until all the stitches are bound off.

THE SIZE IS RIGHT

■ BLOCKING

Like making a gauge swatch, blocking is one of those essential steps that knitters tend to roll their eyes at. It may not be as much fun as choosing colors and textures, and it certainly does not have the meditative rhythm of stitching, but without blocking your perfectly-knit garment will look sloppy. So, please, pull out that blocking equipment and follow along as we teach you the ins and outs (and ups and downs) of molding your knitted pieces into shape.

There are two main categories of blocking: wet and steam. To know which one to use with your particular yarn, consult the Pressing Guide at right. Before beginning either method, gather up any schematics or measurements from the pattern, and use them like architect's plans to know exactly how far the pieces should stretch and where they should dip and swell.

Wet Blocking

With wet blocking, you can either immerse the knitted pieces in cool water, squeeze them out and stretch them to their exact measurements on a flat board, or you can pin the pieces first and then wet them down with a water-filled spray bottle. Which method you choose is largely a matter of personal preference, though you may find the spraying method to be a bit less cumbersome. Once the pieces are wet, walk away and don't fuss with them again until they are completely dry. This may take 24 hours or more, so be patient.

PINNING AND BLOCKING

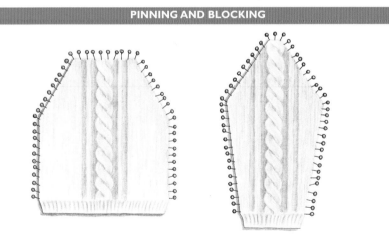

1 Pin the key areas as shown.

2 Pin the piece evenly, omitting the ribbing.

Steam Blocking

To block with steam, first pin the pieces on a flat surface according to the schematics. Fire up your steam iron or handheld steamer, and when it's nice and steamy, hold the iron close to the fabric until the fabric is convincingly damp. DO NOT touch the iron to the stitches; if you must lightly press, protect your knitted investment of time and money by sandwiching a colorfast towel or pressing cloth between the fabric and the hot metal. As with wet blocking, leave the pieces to dry. Drying after steaming probably won't take as long as after wet blocking, but you may still need to be patient for hours on end. In the meantime you can be dreaming up the particulars of your next sweater!

BLOCKING SUPPLIES

1 Flat, covered, padded surface large enough to hold one piece of knitting (e.g. carpet or bed covered with plastic and a towel)

2 Rust-proof T-pins (NOT pins with little plastic colored heads—these will melt during steam blocking, creating a huge mess)

3 Tape measure

4 Spray bottle with cool water (or basin full of cool water) or steam iron (or handheld steamer)

5 Towels (be sure they're colorfast)

6 Pressing cloth

PRESSING GUIDE

Because fibers react differently to heat, it is best to know what to expect before you press or steam them. Just remember that there are many combinations of fibers, and you should choose a process that is compatible with all the components of your yarn. If you are unsure about the fiber content of your yarn, test your gauge swatch before blocking your sweater pieces.

Angora	Wet block by spraying.
Cotton	Wet block or warm/hot steam press.
Linen	Wet block or warm/hot steam press.
Lurex	Do not block.
Mohair	Wet block by spraying.
Novelties	Do not block.
Synthetics	Carefully follow instructions on ball band—usually wet block by spraying, do not press.
Wool and all wool-like fibers (alpaca, camel hair, cashmere)	Wet block by spraying or warm steam press.
Wool blends	Wet block by spraying, do not press unless tested.

SEAMS PERFECT

■ **SEAMING**

Once you've finished off the last strand of every piece of your garment, there's one thing left to do in order to make those pieces into something you can wear: sew them together. In knitting, this sewing together is generally called "seaming," and is accomplished with a yarn needle and the same yarn you used to make your project.

There are many ways to sew together knitted fabric, and each version serves a different purpose. For example, you use one kind of seaming to join adjacent lengths of stockinette stitch, but another to connect vertical and horizontal pieces of the same fabric. Throughout this book we will give you opportunities to practice all of the joining methods presented here. Just follow the pattern instructions to end up with a beautifully finished product and a wide knowledge of seaming.

Before you pick up that needle and thread and start joining little stitches at the hip, you have to make sure you line them up right. To

HOW TO BEGIN SEAMING

If you have left a long tail from your cast-on row, you can use this strand to begin sewing. To make a neat join at the lower edge with no gap, use the technique shown here.

Thread the strand into a yarn needle. With the right sides of both pieces facing you, insert the yarn needle from back to front into the corner stitch of the piece without the tail. Making a figure eight with the yarn, insert the needle from back to front into the stitch with the cast-on tail. Tighten to close the gap.

VERTICAL SEAM ON STOCKINETTE STITCH

The vertical seam is worked from the right side and is used to join two edges row by row. It hides the uneven stitches at the edge of a row and creates an invisible seam, making it appear that the knitting is continuous.

Insert the yarn needle under the horizontal bar between the first and second stitches. Insert the needle into the corresponding bar on the other piece. Continue alternating from side to side.

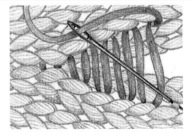

start, find the cast on stitches on both sides. Pin them together with a straight pin or safety pin. Now count up ten rows on each side and pin the corresponding stitches together. Continue in this manner until you get to the top of the two pieces. With a project like a hat, which is worked all in one piece, the rows should line up exactly. If you end up with extra rows on one side at the top, go back and see where they might have sneaked in on the opposite side. When seaming two separate pieces, you may have to ease in extra rows if one piece happens to be slightly longer than the other.

VERTICAL SEAM ON RIBBING

Purl to Purl
When joining ribbing with a purl stitch at each edge, insert the yarn needle under the horizontal bar in the center of a knit stitch on each side in order to keep the pattern continuous.

Knit to Knit
When joining ribbing with a knit stitch at each edge, use the bottom loop of the purl stitch on one side and the top loop of the corresponding purl stitch on the other side.

Purl to Knit
When joining purl and knit stitch edges, skip knit stitch and join two purl stitches as at left.

VERTICAL SEAM ON GARTER STITCH

This seam joins two edges row by row like vertical seaming on stockinette stitch. The alternating pattern of catching top and bottom loops of the stitches makes it so that only you can tell there's a join.

Insert the yarn needle into the top loop on one side, then in the bottom loop of the corresponding stitch on the other side. Continue to alternate in this way.

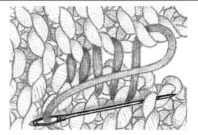

This seam is used to join two bound-off edges, such as for shoulder seams or hoods, and is worked stitch by stitch. You must have the same number of stitches on each piece so that the finished seam will resemble a continuous row of knit stitches. Be sure to pull the yarn tight enough to hide the bound-off edges.

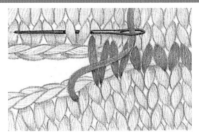

With the bound-off edges together, lined up stitch for stitch, insert the yarn needle under a stitch inside the bound-off edge of one side and then under the corresponding stitch on the other side. Repeat all the way across the join.

Used to connect a bound-off edge to a vertical length of knitted fabric, this seam requires careful pre-measuring and marking to ensure an even seam. Insert the yarn needle under a stitch inside the bound-off edge of the vertical piece.

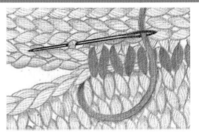

Insert the needle under one or two horizontal bars between the first and second stitches of the horizontal piece. Shown here on Stockinette stitch.

SLIP STITCH CROCHET SEAM

This method creates a visible, though very strong, seam. Use it when you don't mind a bulky join or are looking for an especially sturdy connection.

With the right sides together, insert the crochet hook through both thicknesses. Catch the yarn and draw a loop through. *Insert the hook again. Draw a loop through both thicknesses and the loop on the hook. Repeat from the *, keeping the stitches straight and even.

BACKSTITCH

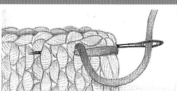

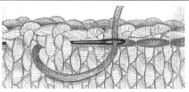

I The backstitch creates a strong, neat, bulky seam that's perfect for extra reinforcement. With the right sides of the pieces facing each other, secure the seam by taking the needle twice around the edges from back to front. Bring the needle up about ¼"/5mm from where the yarn last emerged, as shown.

2 In one motion, insert the needle into the point where the yarn emerged from the previous stitch and back up approximately ¼"/5mm ahead of the emerging yarn. Pull the yarn through. Repeat this step, keeping the stitches straight and even.

PICK UP LINES

▓ PICKING UP STITCHES

So, you're thinking to yourself, what in the world do they mean by "picking up stitches"? First, a definition: picking up stitches means that, with a knitting needle or crochet hook and a new strand of yarn, you dip into and out of the edge of the knitted fabric at hand, creating new loops. These new loops will serve as the foundation for a collar, button band, sleeve or baby bootie instep.

The only two things you need to focus on for picking up stitches along a straight edge are the two S's: side and spacing. For the first "S", be sure to start picking up stitches with the right side facing out. The second "S" reminds you to space the stitches evenly along the fabric. In other words, make sure that the picked up loops aren't clustered together or separated by vast tundras along the knitted edge.

PICKING UP AT VERTICAL EDGE WITH KNITTING NEEDLE

1 Insert the knitting needle into the corner stitch of the first row, one stitch in from the side edge. Wrap the yarn around the needle knitwise.

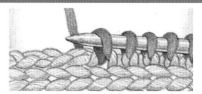

2 Draw the yarn through. You have picked up one stitch. Continue to pick up stitches along the edge. Occasionally skip one row to keep the edge from flaring.

PICKING UP AT HORIZONTAL EDGE WITH CROCHET HOOK

1 Insert the crochet hook from front to back into the center of the first stitch one row below the bound-off edge. Catch the yarn and pull a loop through.

2 Slip the loop onto the knitting needle, being sure it is not twisted. Continue to pick up one stitch in each stitch along the bound-off edge.

LEARNING CURVES

▤ PICKING UP THE NECK

Picking up stitches for a sloped edge (such as for a neck) takes just a little more care than for a straight edge, and most of that care comes in the spacing. When making a neckband, it's especially important that the stitches be picked up evenly so the band will not flare out (too many stitches picked up) or pull in (too few stitches picked up).

MARKING EDGE FOR PICKING UP STITCHES

Stitches must be picked up evenly so that the band will not flare or pull in. Place pins, markers, or yarn, as shown, every 2"/5cm and pick up the same number of stitches between each pair of markers. If you know the number of stitches to be picked up, divide this by the number of sections to determine how many stitches to pick up in each one. If you don't have a final count, use the marked sections to ensure even spacing around the neck.

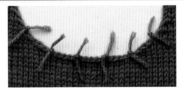

PICKING UP STITCHES ALONG SHAPED EDGE

Stitches picked up along a curved edge. Pick up stitches neatly just inside the shaped edge, following the curve and hiding the jagged selvage.

Stitches picked up along a diagonal edge. Pick up stitches one stitch in from the shaped edge, keeping them in a straight line.

THE HOLE TRUTH

Ever wonder how knitters make those perfect holes along the edges of their cardigans? Well, wonder no more, for we're about to teach you three of the easiest techniques for making beautiful buttonholes: the two-row horizontal buttonhole, the one-row horizontal buttonhole and the yarn over buttonhole. The two-row and one-row buttonholes are shown worked over four stitches, though you might want to use more or fewer depending on the size of your button.

▬ TWO-ROW HORIZONTAL BUTTONHOLE

The two-row horizontal buttonhole is by far the most common buttonhole, and is adaptable to be smaller or larger depending on the size of your button. It is made by binding off a number of stitches on one row and casting them on again on the next. The last stitch bound off is part of the left side of the buttonhole.

TWO-ROW HORIZONTAL BUTTONHOLES

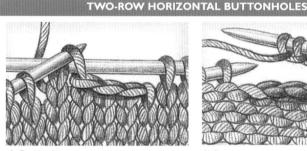 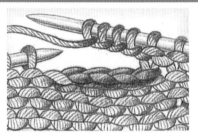

1 On the first row, work to the placement of the buttonhole. Knit two, with the left needle, pull one stitch over the other stitch, *knit one, pull the second stitch over the knit one; repeat from the * twice more. Four stitches have been bound off.

2 On the next row, work to the bound-off stitches and cast on four stitches. On the next row, work these stitches through the back loops to tighten them.

ONE-ROW HORIZONTAL BUTTONHOLE

The one-row horizontal buttonhole is the neatest buttonhole and requires no further reinforcing. Although it's slightly more complicated to work than the two-row horizontal buttonhole, the extra effort produces a fantastic, super-clean result.

YARN OVER BUTTONHOLE

The yarn over buttonhole produces an especially small space in the fabric, and is used mostly in children's garments. This buttonhole is accomplished by knitting two stitches together, followed by a yarn over (see page 42). On the return row, work the yarn over as if it is a stitch.

(see page 42)

TIP

Debating about how many buttons to use? Always err on the side of more. The smaller the gaps between buttons, the flatter and smoother your cardigan band will appear. It's a good idea to buy the buttons for your project before you start knitting so that you'll have an idea of the size, spacing and number of buttonholes on the buttonhole band.

ONE-ROW HORIZONTAL BUTTONHOLE

I Work to the buttonhole, bring yarn to front, and slip a stitch purlwise. Place yarn at back and leave it there. *Slip next stitch from left needle. Pass the first slipped stitch over it; repeat from the * three times more (not moving yarn). Slip the last bound-off stitch to left needle and turn work.

2 Using the cable cast-on with the yarn at the back, cast on five stitches as follows: *Insert the right needle between the first and second stitches on the left needle, draw up a loop, place the loop on the left needle; repeat from the * four times more, turn the work.

3 Slip the first stitch with the yarn in back from the left needle and pass the extra cast-on stitch over it to close the buttonhole. Work to the end of the row.

■ BUTTONHOLE SPACING

To get your buttonholes as evenly spaced as possible, start by placing markers on the button band for the first and last buttonholes. Measure the distance between them and place markers evenly for the remaining buttonholes.

To make sure your buttons and buttonholes line up exactly in the end, use this easy tip: Count the number of rows between the lower edge and the first marker, between the first and second markers, and so on. Make a note of how many rows separate each marker, and then make your buttonholes on the corresponding rows of the buttonhole band.

TIP

Although most patterns call for the button and buttonhole bands to be worked separately and sewn on later, you can also work the front bands with the main piece on some styles. This simple time-saving technique eliminates the need for extra seaming, and allows you to space the buttonholes precisely along the edge of the sweater.

YARN OVER

Between two knit stitches.
Bring the yarn from the back of the work to the front between the two needles. Knit the next stitch, bringing the yarn to the back over the right needle as shown.

BUTTON UP

To sew on buttons, you can use yarn (if it goes through the button) or matching thread. When sewing on metal buttons, which tend to cut the thread, you may wish to use waxed dental floss. Double the thread and tie a knot on the end. Then slip your button onto the needle and thread. You can further secure the button with a square of fabric or felt at the back, which is especially desirable on garments that receive heavy wear, such as jackets.

SEWING ON BUTTONS

Knotted thread has a tendency to pull through knit fabric. Lock it in place by inserting thread into fabric on the right side and through the doubled thread as shown here. Clip knotted end.

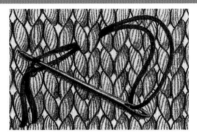

■ ACCESSORIES

When you're first learning to knit, there's not much you need besides two knitting needles and a couple balls of yarn. Once you move onto more advanced projects, however, you may find some of these inexpensive gadgets infinitely helpful.

Scissors

We think it goes without saying that knitters need scissors. The ones that work best are small, with sharp points that allow you to get close to the work when snipping off loose ends. Be sure to cover those sharp points with a travel case if you'll be toting them around town.

Yarn needles

Also called "tapestry needles," these are the blunt-tipped, large-eyed needles used for seaming and weaving in ends. Most yarn needles are made out of metal or plastic.

Tape Measure

Like the yarn needle, a tape measure is an essential knitting accessory. Buy one that is flexible but won't stretch (fiberglass is best), and that has both inches and centimeters marked on it. Since measuring is such an important part of knitting a garment, be sure to replace your tape measure once it starts to look worn.

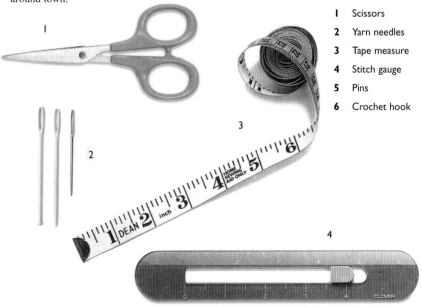

1	Scissors
2	Yarn needles
3	Tape measure
4	Stitch gauge
5	Pins
6	Crochet hook

Stitch Gauge

This flat rectangle of metal or plastic simplifies the process of measuring gauge by providing a little window through which you can easily count stitches. To use it, lay your knitting down on a flat surface and then line up the L-shaped window with the corner of a stitch. Count the number of Vs in the window (both horizontally and vertically) to get accurate stitch and row gauges.

Stitch gauges also offer another handy feature—a row of holes that can be used to identify size on unmarked needles. To use this feature, simply slip the needle into holes of increasing size until you reach one that allows the needle to pass all the way through. The hole's corresponding number is your needle's size.

Pins

Without pins, you'll have a hard time seaming or blocking your finished pieces. Choose a variety of straight pins and safety pins to suit every situation. Straight pins with colored heads (metal, not plastic) are easy to see against knitted work when seaming, rust-proof T-pins are necessary for blocking, and safety pins can do everything from holding together pieces to be seamed to marking numbers of rows and holding small numbers of set-aside stitches.

Crochet Hooks

You don't have to be a master crocheter to find these little hook-ended sticks extremely helpful. Crochet hooks have a variety of uses in knitting, like seaming with slip stitches,

4

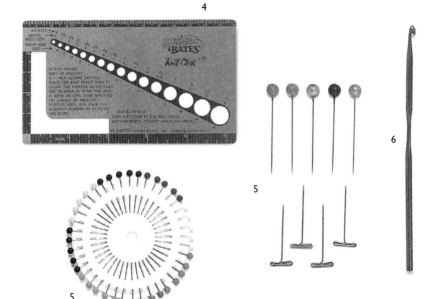

6

5

5

making decorative edgings and even picking up stitches. Like knitting needles, they come in a variety of sizes and materials to suit every yarn thickness and knitter's taste.

Stitch Holders

These gems hold your open stitches, preventing them from unraveling. Stitch holders come in a range of sizes and shapes, though most are made of metal or plastic. The size you'll probably use the most are medium-sized ones (approximately 4-6"/10-15cm). For fewer stitches use a large safety pin; if you need to place an enormous number of stitches on hold, it might be easier to thread them onto a length of contrasting yarn.

Row Counters

If you want your front and back pieces to match up exactly, or if you need to document rows passed in a complicated pattern, row counters are a lifesaver. You can choose from several styles: small cylinders that fit at the bottom of your needles, push-button squares with number dials and even tiny pegboards that keep track of shaping and patterns at the same time. If you prefer a pencil and paper, try pasting a sticky note to your patterns and marking off each row as you go along.

Stitch Markers

Great for remembering where to increase and decrease, or for flagging the beginning of a circular row, these accessories can make the difference between headway and a headache. Some stitch markers come in the form of miniature rubber donuts that slip over the needle, while others have slits that make it possible to attach the markers to the knitting

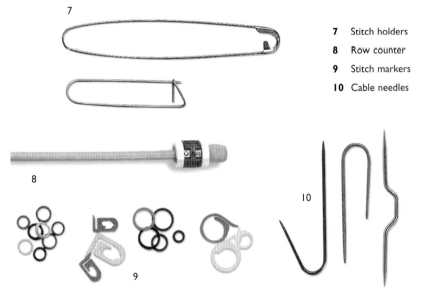

7

7 Stitch holders

8 Row counter

9 Stitch markers

10 Cable needles

8

10

9

itself. If you don't have any stitch markers on hand, a short piece of contrasting yarn tied into a loop will also do the trick.

Cable needles

J-hook, straight pin or straight pin with a bend? It's your choice when it comes to cable needles. The basic premise of this helper is a two-pointed needle that holds stitches temporarily while you work another portion of a cable pattern. You'll find them in metal, plastic, wood or bone. Whatever the material, there are generally three size gradations for different weight yarns.

Pompom Makers

If you want your pompoms to be especially uniform and quick-to-make, try these plastic disks with missing centers. Because there are many variations on the basic pompom maker,

follow the directions on your individual package to get the best result.

Point Protectors

If you ever come back to your knitting and discover that a good number of the stitches have fallen off the end of the needle, you'll understand the reason behind these little plastic cones. Place one on the end of each needle to stop your knitting from running away with itself. Point protectors come in a few different sizes to accommodate a range of needle sizes.

Bobbins

When making a sweater using more than one color, bobbins are indispensable. Wind lengths of yarn in each color around these plastic holders, then use them like you would small-scale balls of yarn. Most bobbins are

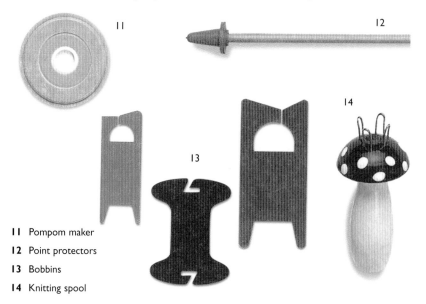

11 Pompom maker

12 Point protectors

13 Bobbins

14 Knitting spool

configured so that the yarn won't unwind while you work. Just like everything else, bobbins come in a couple of different sizes so that you don't have to wind super bulky yarn around a bobbin meant for a super fine yarn.

Knitting Spools

These four-pronged contraptions might spark a flashback to summer camp as they are often the first exposure that children have to knitting (remember making potholders and friendship bracelets?). Adult variations produce knitted braids, which can be used in a variety of ways to decorate or pull together a project.

Notebook

It's always a good idea to keep a record of everything you knit. Compiling your patterns, yarn samples and measurements into a durable notebook can help you not only when you want to recreate the same project, but also when you want to show off your knitting accomplishments to your friends and family.

Knitting Bag

It doesn't have to look like a knitting bag (or even be labeled as such) to be a dynamite yarn and project carrier. A few things you might look for in a potential knitting satchel are: a small pocket to hold accessories, comfortable handles or straps and a secure closure to keep dust and dirt out and all of your supplies in.

FOR MORE INFORMATION

This book teaches the very basics of knitting, and is a great resource to get you started. As you gain more experience, you may find you need a more comprehensive guide. For intermediate and advanced knitters, we recommend the *Vogue Knitting Ultimate Knitting Book* and *Vogue Knitting Quick Reference Ultimate Portable Knitting Compendium.* Order these titles through your local yarn store or call (800) 298-1032.

STARTER KNITS

Learning how to knit takes practice, practice, practice, and this garter stitch scarf designed by Cara Beckerich helps you do just that. Get the hang of knitting consecutive rows quickly using big needles and chunky yarn. And revel in the fact that because of its multiple colors and thick-and-thin texture, this yarn won't tell if you happen to drop a stitch or make an accidental knot. Most of all, have fun. You're knitting now!

KNITTED MEASUREMENTS
Approx 10" x 60"/25.5 x 152cm

MATERIALS
▪ 2 3½oz/100g balls (each approx 55yd/50m) of Colinette Yarns/Unique Kolours *Point 5* (wool) in #134 (**6**)

▪ One pair size 35 (19mm) needles *or size to obtain gauge*

GAUGE
6 sts and 4 rows to 4"/10cm over garter st using size 35 (19mm) needles.
Take time to check gauge.

SCARF
Cast on 15 sts. Work in garter st (k every row) until piece measures 60"/152cm or until you run out of yarn. Bind off. Weave in ends.

TIP
When you're buying yarn for a project, always be sure to match the dye lot numbers on each ball band, and to buy enough of one dye lot to see you through the entire project. Different dye lots of the same color yarn can vary drastically, and it's always better to have yarn left over rather than a project that spans many different shades.

FUR SURE

Once you feel confident with the process of knitting, try your hand at keeping an even tension and adding a simple embellishment with fur or faux fur. The slightly smaller needle size and even-textured yarn clearly illustrate the ridges of garter stitch, giving you a chance to see how much you've learned already. Designed by Sandi Prosser.

KNITTED MEASUREMENTS
Approx 9" x 48"/ 23 x 122cm, excluding fur edging

MATERIALS
▥ 6 1¾oz/50g balls (each approx 60yd/55m) of Lion Brand *Kool Wool* (wool/acrylic) in #186 melon (⑤)
▥ 2yd/2m Skacel Collection *Pelligo* (rabbit hair)
▥ If using faux fur: Mokuba Art. #1516 in black
▥ One pair size 10 (6mm) needles *or size to obtain gauge*
▥ Size K/10.5 (7mm) crochet hook

GAUGE
13 sts and 23 rows to 4"/10cm over garter st using size 10 (6mm) needles.
Take time to check gauge.

SCARF
Cast on 30 sts. Work in garter st (k every row) until piece measures 48"/122cm from beg. Bind off. Weave in ends.

FUR TRIM
(Optional)
With crochet hook, work 1 sc (single crochet) in each stitch along edges. See page 77 for crochet techique.

TIP
Try these two easy tips for making your knitting tension as even as possible:
1. Keep the stitches to be worked as close to the tip of the left-hand needle as possible without having them fall off. This prevents the yarn from being stretched.
2. Wrap the working strand around the pinky and index fingers of your "throwing" hand to increase tautness of the yarn, making uniform stitches easier to create.

MAKE IT EASY

Combine alternating rows of knit and purl stitches to make this fun and funky scarf. Used also in "Instant Success" (see page 52), this thick-and-thin yarn is very forgiving of the occasional mistake. Enjoy the fast-paced thrill and mind-relaxing rhythm of learning the most popular stitch pattern in knitting.

KNITTED MEASUREMENTS
Approx 9½" x 48"/24 x 122cm

MATERIALS
▓ 6 3½oz/100g balls (each approx 55yd/50m) of Colinette Yarns/Unique Kolours *Point 5* (wool) in #134 (6)
▓ One pair size 15 (10mm) needles *or size to obtain gauge*

GAUGE
10 sts and 12 rows to 4"/10cm over St st using size 15 (10mm) needles.
Take time to check gauge.

SCARF
Cast on 23 sts. Work in Stockinette st (k 1 row, p 1 row) until piece measures 48"/ 122cm or until you run out of yarn. Bind off. Weave in ends.

TIP
There are many ways to exercise your creativity with knitting, and one way is to make the same project using different yarns (also called substitution). For best results, use the Standardized Yarn Weight System Chart on page 13 to select a yarn that is the same weight as the original recommendation.

RIB IT

You've graduated! Combining knit and purl stitches together in the same row to make a rib pattern is definitely a sign that you're on your way. Don't forget to move the yarn back and forth in between the different stitches, and enjoy the finished product of this endeavor: a stylish, reversible scarf that is incredibly satisfying to make. Designed by Veronica Manno.

KNITTED MEASUREMENTS
Approx 7" x 44"/18 x 122cm

MATERIALS
▦ 1 3½oz/100g balls (each approx 219yd/200m) of Rowany Yarns *Rowanspun Aran* (wool) in #972 green **(4)**
▦ One pair size 9 (5.5mm) needles *or size to obtain gauge*

GAUGE
20 sts and 23 rows to 4"/10cm over k4, p4 rib (slightly stretched) using size 9 (5.5mm) needles.
Take time to check gauge.

K4, P4 RIB
(multiple of 8 sts)
Row 1 (RS) *K4, p4; rep from * to end.
Row 2 K the knit and p the purl sts.
Rep row 2 for k4, p4 rib.

SCARF
Cast on 36 sts. Work in k4, p4 rib until piece measures 44"/122cm from beg or until you run out of yarn. Bind off. Weave in ends.

TIP
Since ribbing is elastic and tends to "spring" towards the middle of the fabric, it can be challenging to take its gauge accurately. To remedy this situation, stretch the fabric slightly before measuring and be sure to include the exposed purl stitches in your count.

COLOR PLAY

The marriage of horizontal stripes and vertical ribs in this scarf designed by Charlotte Parry, make for a stunning visual effect and provide the perfect opportunity to refine your ability to join yarn and make ribs. Hint: Learn to carry unused colors up the side of the work, and in the process cut out much of the work of weaving in ends.

KNITTED MEASUREMENTS
Approx 9" x 40"/23 x 101.5cm

MATERIALS
▦ 2 1¾oz/50g balls (each approx 61yd/55m) of Lang/Berroco, Inc. *Polar Color* (wool) each in #0079 blue (A), #0048 pink (B) and #0097 green (C) (⑤)

▦ One pair size 9 (5.5mm) needles *or size to obtain gauge*

GAUGE
26 sts and 22 rows to 4"/10cm over rib pat (slightly stretched) using size 9 (5.5mm) needles.
Take time to check gauge.

K2, P2 RIB
(multiple of 4 sts plus 2 extra)
Row 1 (RS) K2, *p2, k2; rep from * to end.
Row 2 K the knit and p the purl sts.
Rep row 2 for k2, p2 rib.

STRIPE PATTERN
Working in rib pat, *2 rows A, 2 rows B, 2 rows C; rep from * (6 rows) for stripe pat.

SCARF
With A, cast on 58 sts. Work in k2, p2 rib and stripe pat until piece measures 40"/101.5cm from beg. Bind off. Weave in ends.

TIP
To carry non-working colors of a stripe pattern up the side of the scarf, follow these easy instructions: When you've finished working with one color and are about to work the next color, bring the two unworked strands up the side of the work and pick them both up from underneath the working strand. The working strand will catch the carried strands, making a neat, clean edge.

TINY TOPPER

Start a little one off in style with this adorable hat designed by Veronica Manno. The project's simple shaping and easy seaming offer the perfect opportunity to venture away from knitting only in squares and rectangles. In addition, the luxurious yarn and small size make it a joy to stitch from start to quick finish.

SIZE
Instructions are written for Newborn.

KNITTED MEASUREMENTS
▥ Head circumference 16½"/42cm

MATERIALS
▥ 1 1¾oz/50g balls (each approx 135yd/125m) of Debbie Bliss/KFI *Baby Cashmerino* (wool/microfibre/cashmere) in #600 pink **(2)**
▥ One pair size 4 (3.5mm) needles *or size to obtain gauge*

GAUGE
24 sts and 32 rows to 4"/10cm over St st using size 4 (3.5mm) needles.
Take time to check gauge.

K2, P2 RIB
(multiple of 4 sts)
Row 1 (RS) *K2, p2; rep from * to end.
Row 2 K the knit and p the purl sts.
Rep row 2 for k2, p2 rib.

HAT
Cast on 96 sts. Work in k2, p2 rib for ¾"/2cm. **Next row (RS)** Work in St st (k 1 row, p 1 row), inc 3 sts evenly across using bar increase—99 sts. Cont in St st until piece measures 3½"/9cm from beg.
Shape top
Next row (RS) *K7, k2tog; rep from * to end—88 sts. Work 1 row even.
Next row (RS) *K6, k2tog; rep from * to end—77 sts. Work 1 row even.
Next row (RS) *K5, k2tog; rep from * to end—66 sts. Work 1 row even.
Next row (RS) *K4, k2tog; rep from * to end—55 sts. Work 1 row even.
Next row (RS) *K3, k2tog; rep from * to end—44 sts. Work 1 row even.
Next row (RS) *K2, k2tog; rep from * to end—33 sts. Work 1 row even.
Next row (RS) *K1, k2tog; rep from * to end—22 sts. Work 1 row even.
Next row (RS) *K2tog; rep from * to end—11 sts.
Cut yarn, leaving a long tail for sewing. Thread tail through yarn needle and pass it through each st, pulling tightly to close the top. Sew back seam using both vertical seam on ribbing (purl to knit) and on stockinette stitch.

PURPLE REIGNS

Hats off to Carla Scott, the designer of this chunky head warmer. The variegated yarn's colors fleck and change without any extra help from you, and the inherent stretch of the rib pattern make this hat fit perfectly on almost any adult. When it comes time to seam, gain valuable experience sewing ribs without breaking the pattern.

SIZE
Instructions are written for one size and pulls in or stretches to fit most adults.

KNITTED MEASUREMENTS
Head circumference (slightly stretched) 18"/45.5cm

MATERIALS
▥ 2 3½oz/100g balls (each approx 110yd/100m) of Naturwolle/Muench Yarns *Black Forest Yarn* (wool) in #12 soft (■4■)
▥ One pair size 8 (5mm) needles *or size to obtain gauge*

GAUGE
16 sts and 24 rows to 4"/10cm over k4, p4 rib (slightly stretched) using size 8 (5mm) needles.
Take time to check gauge.

K4, P4 RIB
(multiple of 8 sts)
Row 1 (RS) *K4, p4; rep from * to end.
Row 2 K the knit and p the purl sts.
Rep row 2 for k4, p4 rib.

HAT
Cast on 72 sts. Work in k4, p4 rib for 8"/20.5cm
Shape top
Row 1 (RS) *K1, k2tog, k1, p1, p2tog, p1; rep from *to end—54 sts.
Row 2 K the knit and p the purl sts.
Row 3 *K2tog, k1, p2tog, p1; rep from * to end—36 sts.
Row 4 K the knit and p the purl sts.
Row 5 *K2tog, p2; rep from * to end—27 sts.
Row 6 K the knit and p the purl sts.
Row 7 *K1, p2 tog; rep from * to end—18 sts.
Row 8 K the knit and p the purl sts.
Row 9 *K2tog; rep from* to end—9 sts.
Cut yarn leaving a long tail for sewing. Thread tail through yarn needle and pass it through each st, pulling tightly to close the top. Sew back seam using vertical seam on ribbing (purl to knit). Weave in ends.

EARN YOUR STRIPES

In knitting, making your first sweater is a milestone. It says: "Not only can I put together yarn and needles, but I can do it well enough to make my own clothes!" This super-easy introduction to creating a sweater uses garter stitch and minimal shaping so that you can focus on learning to assemble the finished pieces. In the process, pick up a handy trick for shoulder seaming: the three-needle bind-off. Designed by Kristin Spurkland.

SIZES

Instructions are written for size Small. Changes for Medium, Large and X-Large are in parentheses.

KNITTED MEASUREMENTS

▥ Bust 35 (39, 43, 47)"/89 (99, 109, 119)cm
▥ Length 20¼ (21, 21¾, 22½)"/51.5 (53.5, 55, 57)cm
▥ Upper arm 16½ (17½, 18½, 19½)"/42 (44, 47, 50)cm

MATERIALS

▥ 3 (3, 4, 4) 3½oz/100g balls (each approx 127yd/117m) of Classic Elite Yarns *Montera* (wool/llama) each in #3887 lime green (A), #3831 aqua (B) and #3856 blue (C) (▣)
▥ One pair size 9 (5.5mm) needles *or size to obtain gauge*
▥ Stitch holders

GAUGE

16 sts and 32 rows to 4"/10cm over garter st using size 9 (5.5mm) needles.
Take time to check gauge.

STRIPE PATTERN

Working in garter st, *2 rows A, 2 rows B, 2 rows C; rep from * (6 rows) for stripe pat.

Carry yarn not in use along side of work. (See page 61 for details).

BACK

With A, cast on 70 (78, 86, 94) sts. Work in stripe pat until piece measures 20¼ (21, 21¾, 22½)"/51.5 (53.5, 55, 57)cm from beg, or 27 (28, 29, 30) stripe pat rep, end with 2 rows C.

Next rows (RS) With A, k 12 (14, 16, 18) sts and place a holder for one shoulder, bind off center 46 (50, 54, 58) sts for neck, k to end and place rem 12 (14, 16, 18) sts on a 2nd holder for other shoulder.

FRONT

Work as for back.

SLEEVES

With A, cast on 34 (36, 38, 40) sts. Work in stripe pat for 2½"/6.5cm. Cont in stripe pat, AT SAME TIME, inc 1 st each side of this row, then every 6th row 3 (7, 8, 12) times more, every 8th row 12 (9, 9, 6) times—66 (70, 74, 78) sts. Work even until sleeve measures 18 (18, 18¾, 18¾)"/

45.5 (45.5, 47.5, 47.5)cm from beg, or 24 (24, 25, 25) stripe pat rep. Bind off with C.

FINISHING

Block pieces to measurements. Join shoulder seams using Three-Needle Bind-off. Place markers at 8¼ (8¾, 9¼, 9¾)"/21 (22, 23.5, 25)cm down from shoulders. Sew sleeves to armholes between markers using vertical to horizontal seam. Sew side and sleeve seams using vertical seam on garter stitch.

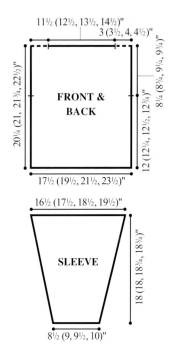

11½ (12½, 13½, 14½)"

3 (3½, 4, 4½)"

8¼ (8¾, 9¼, 9¾)"

20¼ (21, 21¾, 22½)"

FRONT & BACK

12 (12¼, 12½, 12¾)"

17½ (19½, 21½, 23½)"

16½ (17½, 18½, 19½)"

SLEEVE

18 (18, 18¾, 18¾)"

8½ (9, 9½, 10)"

SHAKE YOUR BOOTIE

Now you're cruising! With knitting, purling, ribbing, decreasing, increasing and seaming all under your belt, you're well on your way to becoming a knitting pro. So, how would you like to cinch that title by learning to pick up stitches, work double decreases and even dye yarn with powdered drink mix? Well, hang on because we're about to do all three with these delightful baby booties designed by Jean Guirguis.

SIZES
Instructions are written for size Newborn. Changes for 3 months and 6 months are in parentheses.

MATERIALS
▦ 1 ball 100% wool worsted weight yarn in white (**4**)
▦ One pair size 5 (3.75mm) needles *or size to obtain gauge*
▦ Stitch holders
▦ 1 package strawberry powered drink mix
▦ 1yd/1m ½"/13mm wide grosgrain ribbon

GAUGE
24 sts and 47 rows to 4"/10cm over garter st using size 5 (3.75mm) needles.
Take time to check gauge.

See preparing yarn and dyeing instructions on pages 72-73.

CUFF
Cast on 25 sts and work in garter st (k every row) for 5 (5¾, 6½)"/13 (14.5, 16.5)cm. Bind off. Along one long side, pick up and k30 (34, 38) sts and work in garter st for 10 (12, 14) rows. Cut yarn.

Instep
Next row (RS) Place first and last 10 (12, 14) sts on a holder and work 11 (13, 13)

rows in garter st over center 10 sts. Cut yarn. **Next row (RS)** Work 10 (12, 14) sts from right holder, pick up and k7 (8, 9) sts along side of instep, work center 10 sts on needle, pick up and k7 (8, 9) sts along other side of instep, work 10 (12, 14) sts from left holder—44 (50, 56) sts. K next row, inc 1 st each side of center 10 sts—46 (52, 58) sts. Cont in garter st for 10 (12, 14) rows.

Sole
Next row (RS) K3 (4, 5), SK2P, k11 (12, 13), k3tog, k6 (8, 10), SK2P, k11 (12, 13), k3tog, k3 (4, 5)—38 (44, 50) sts. K 1 row.
Next row (RS) K2 (3, 4), SK2P, k9 (10, 11), k3tog, k4 (6, 8), SK2P, k9 (10, 11), k3tog, k2 (3, 4)—30 (36, 42) sts. K 1 row.
Next row (RS) K1 (2, 3), SK2P, k7 (8, 9), k3tog, k2 (4, 6), SK2P, k7 (8, 9), k3tog, k1 (2, 3)—22 (28, 34) sts.
For size 6 months only
K 1 row. **Next row** K2, SK2P, k7, k3tog, k4, SK2P, k7, k3tog, k2—26 sts.
For all sizes K 2 rows.

FINISHING
Divide sts on two needles and join tog using Three-Needle Bind-off. Sew back seam using vertical seam on garters stitch. Using grosgrain ribbon, fashion a bow and attach to instep of bootie.

With the help of powdered fruit drink mix, knitters who might never venture into the complicated, often messy, world of yarn dyeing can make their own unique creations without all of the fuss. The key is to use your imagination (and the vast collection of flavors) to come up with your perfect color, and then dye away.

■ PREPARING YARN

Depending on what kind of yarn you purchase, it may be packaged as a ball or a hank. The major difference between the two is that the ball is already wound into a knitter-friendly package, while the hank needs some preparation before you can work from it. There are some instances, however, when you actually need a hank instead of a ball (such as for yarn dyeing, here). Follow these fun instructions for transforming a hank into a ball, or vise versa.

To make a center-pull ball from a hank, first un-kink the hank so that it looks like a giant oval of yarn. Remove any knots or ties from the oval, and then place it either over the back of a chair or around the hands of a willing yarn-winding participant. Find one end of the skein and unwind about two feet from the chair back or hands.

Lay the yarn across the palm of your hand, leaving a six-inch tail at the end to form the pull string. Wrap the yarn from the hank in a figure-8 around your thumb and pinky finger approximately ten times, and then gently remove the 8-shaped yarn from your fingers. Be sure to keep your thumb on the pull string so it doesn't get "lost" in the wound yarn. Position your first and middle fingers on the outside of the small wad of yarn, and start wrapping in loose circles around your fingers and the wad. When you've wrapped enough to make a solid ball formation, remove your fingers and keep wrapping around and around until all of the yarn is out of the oval and into the ball (again, make sure you keep your thumb on that pull string so you don't lose it!) When your ball starts to look lopsided, simply turn it around and wrap in a different direction. To use the ball, gently tug on the pull string; the yarn should come out smoothly and easily, without causing the whole ball to roll around on the floor.

In the event that you need to turn a ball back into a hank, start by finding an end on your ball (either in the center or on the outside). If you have a willing assistant, ask that person to hold their arms outstretched and shoulder-width apart with palms facing. The yarn assistant should grasp the yarn's end between his or her thumb and index finger as you start to wrap in that characteristic oval shape around his or her hands. After a certain amount of wrapping the assistant will be able to let go of the end and the oval will stay in place. Continue wrapping until all of the yarn is in a hank. If you don't have anyone else around who's willing to hold your yarn, a chair back will work. Just use a piece of removable clear tape to anchor the yarn end to the chair back, and wrap in an oval, just like you would around hands.

HERE'S HOW

YARN DYEING

MATERIALS

▓ 1 hank 100% wool (worsted weight) yarn in white (NOT superwash/machine washable or acrylic/acrylic mix)

▓ 1 package powdered fruit drink mix in the color of your choice (strawberry was used here).

▓ Pair of rubber gloves

▓ Plastic hanger

▓ White vinegar

▓ Measuring cup

▓ Small cup

▓ Teaspoon

▓ Small amount of dish soap

▓ The kitchen sink works well for dyeing the yarn.

DIRECTIONS

1 Pour contents from one powdered fruit drink mix package into a small cup of warm water and set aside to dissolve. Use no more than ¼ cup water; the solution should be highly concentrated.

2 Put on the gloves and hold the hank of yarn under running lukewarm water to thoroughly wet yarn.

3 Squeeze extra water out of the yarn and lay it in an oval shape in the bottom of the sink.

4 Pour the powdered fruit drink solution over the yarn in an "S" motion,

distributing the dye unevenly so as to create the space-dyed effect.

5 Leave the powdered fruit drink mix on the yarn for 15-20 minutes to set.

6 After the dye has set, place the hank under cold running water so that the excess dye runs out. Switch to lukewarm water and continue to rinse until water runs clear.

7 Fill the sink 2"/5cm deep with lukewarm water and add ¼ cup vinegar. Place hank in vinegar solution and leave for ten minutes to set dye.

8 Drain the sink and rinse the hank well with lukewarm water. Use a small of amount of liquid dish soap and wash the hank well to rid it of the vinegar odor. Finish with a cold water rinse.

9 Hang hank around the neck of a plastic hanger and allow to dry in the shower. After about 24 hours (or when the hank has completely dried), remove it from the hanger and wind back into a ball.

BABY BASIC

Now that you've made your very first sweater, it's time to hone your skills—with a few new twists. By learning how to read schematics for an open-front sweater, shape a neck, add a decorative crochet edging and sew on buttons, you'll cement your foundation of sweater assembly with this charming baby cardigan designed by Veronica Manno.

SIZES
Instructions are written for size 6 months. Changes for 12 and 18 months are in parentheses.

KNITTED MEASUREMENTS
▪ Chest (buttoned) 22 (24¼, 26½)"/56 (61.5, 67)cm
▪ Length 8½ (9½, 10½)"/21.5 (24, 26.5)cm
▪ Upper arm 7 (8, 9)"/18 (20.5, 23)cm

MATERIALS
▪ 2 1¾oz/50g balls (each approx 98yd/90m) of Karabella Yarns *Aurora 8 Ply* (wool) in #25 pink (MC) (◼3◼)
▪ 1 ball in #1350 off white (CC)
▪ One pair size 7 (4.5mm) needles *or size to obtain gauge*
▪ Size G/6 (4mm)crochet hook
▪ Three ½"/13mm buttons

GAUGE
19 sts and 30 rows to 4"/10cm over St st using size 7 (4.5mm) needles.
Take time to check gauge.

BACK
With MC, cast on 52 (56, 60) sts. Work in St st until piece measures 8½ (9½, 10½)"/21.5 (24, 26.5)cm from beg. Bind off all sts.

LEFT FRONT
With MC, cast on 24 (28, 32) sts. Work in St st until piece measures 7 (8, 9)"/18 (20.5, 23)cm from beg, end with a RS row.
Neck shaping
Next row (WS) Bind off 4 (4, 6) sts (neck edge), work to end. Cont to bind off at neck edge 3 (4, 4) sts twice, 2 sts once. Work even until same length as back. Bind off rem 12 (14, 16) sts for shoulder.

RIGHT FRONT
Work as for left front, reversing neck shaping by ending the last row before the neck shaping with a WS row and work as foll:
Neck shaping
Next row (RS) Bind off 4 (4, 6) sts (neck edge), work to end. Cont to work neck decs at beg of RS rows as for left front.

SLEEVES

With MC, cast on 28 (30, 34) sts. Work in St st, inc 1 st each side every 10th (8th, 8th) row 3 (4, 4) times—34 (38, 42) sts. Work even until piece measures 5 (5½, 6)"/12.5 (14, 15)cm from beg. Bind off.

FINISHING

Block pieces to measurements. Sew shoulder seams. Place markers 3½ (4, 4½)"/9 (10, 11.5)cm down from shoulders on front and back. Sew sleeves between markers. Sew side and sleeve seams. With RS facing, crochet hook and CC, work 1 row sc around lower, front and neck edges. Do not turn. Working from left to right, work 1 row reverse sc in each sc. Fasten off. Work in same way around lower edge of each sleeve. To work 3 buttonholes on right front, work, ch 3, skip 1 st for each buttonhole, place the first at top of neck and 2 others spaced 2"/5cm apart.

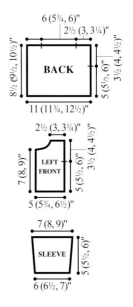

ON THE EDGE

■ CROCHET EDGINGS

One of the best ways to neaten up and add style to the edges of a knitted garment is to use crochet, a close cousin of knitting that employs one hook instead of two needles to accomplish its task. Work one or two rows of single crochet to hide uneven edges, or add a row of reverse single crochet for an especially decorative finish.

SINGLE CROCHET (SC)

One row of single crochet makes a neat, narrow edge; several rows form a firm edge. You can also use it as a base for other crochet edges.

1 Insert hook into a stitch and draw up a loop, bring the yarn over the hook, and pull it through the first loop. *Insert the hook into the next stitch and draw through a second loop.

2 Yarn over and pull through both loops on the hook. Repeat from the * to the end.

REVERSE SINGLE CROCHET (SC)

Work a reverse single crochet edge the same as a single crochet, but from left to right rather than right to left.

1 Pull through a loop on the left edge. Chain one. *Go into the next stitch to the right. Catch the yarn as shown and pull it through the fabric, then underneath (not through) the loop on the hook.

2 Bring the yarn over the top of the crochet hook and around as shown, then draw the yarn through both loops. Repeat from the *.

YOUNGER SET

Who could resist this coordinating set of winter warmers? With this trio of projects you'll practice lots of valuable skills, such as working a button band with the main piece, making yarn over buttonholes, picking up stitches for a neck and making pompoms. Designed by Jean Guirguis.

SIZES

Cardigan

Instructions are written for size 6 months. Changes for 12 and 18 months are in parentheses.

Hat

Instructions are written for size 6 months. Changes for 12-18 months are in parentheses

KNITTED MEASUREMENTS

CARDIGAN

▥ Chest (buttoned) 22½ (25, 27)"/57 (63.5, 68.5) cm
▥ Length 10½ (11½, 12½)"/26.5 (29, 32)cm
▥ Upper arm 9 (10, 11)"/23 (25.5, 28)cm

HAT

Head circumference 17 (18½)"/43 (47)cm

MATERIALS

▥ 2 (3, 3) 4oz/113g balls (each approx 125yd/114m) of Brown Sheep Company *Lambs Pride Bulky* (wool/mohair) each in #M57 blue (A) and #M100 purple (B) (**5**)
▥ One pair size 10 (6mm) needles *or size to obtain gauge*
▥ Five ¾"/20mm buttons

GAUGE

13 sts and 20 rows to 4"/10cm over St st using size 10 (6mm) needles.
Take time to check gauge.

K1, P1 RIB

Row 1 (RS) *K1, p1; rep from * to end.
Row 2 K the knit and p the purl sts.
Rep row 2 for k1, p1 rib.

STRIPE PATTERN
*2 rows B, 2 rows A; rep from * (4 rows) for stripe pat.

CARDIGAN

BACK
With A, cast on 36 (39, 42) sts. Work in k1, p1 rib for 1"/2.5cm. Work in St st and stripe pat until piece measures 10½ (11½, 12½)"/26.5 (29, 32)cm from beg. Bind off.

NOTE
Buttonholes are worked on left front for boy's version. If working a girl's version, work buttonholes on the right front.

LEFT FRONT
With A, cast on 17 (19, 21) (20, 22) sts. Work in k1, p1 rib for 2 rows. Work yo buttonholes (see page 42) as foll:
Next (buttonhole) row (RS)
Work to last 4 sts, p1, k2tog, yo, k1. Cont in rib, working yo as a st, until piece measures 1"/2.5cm from beg.

Next row (RS) Work in St st and stripe pat to last 4 sts, change to A and cont k1, p1 rib (buttonhole band) to end. Cont as established, working 4 more buttonholes spaced 1¼ (2, 2¼)"/4.5 (5, 5.5)cm apart. Work even until piece measures 8 (9, 10)"/20.5 (23, 25.5)cm from beg, end with a RS row.
Neck shaping
Next row (WS) Bind off 3 (4, 5) sts (neck edge), work to end. Cont to bind off at neck edge 2 sts once, 1 st 3 times. Work even until same length as back. Bind off rem 9 (10, 11) sts for shoulder.

RIGHT FRONT
Work as for left front, reversing placement of front band (omit buttonholes) as foll:
Next row (RS) Cont rib over first 4 sts, work in St st and stripe pat to end. Reverse neck shaping, ending last row before neck shaping with a WS row, and work as foll:
Next row (RS) Bind off 3 (4, 5) sts (neck edge), work to end. Complete to correspond to left front.

SLEEVES

With A, cast on 19 (21, 24) sts. Work in k1, p1 rib for 1"/2.5cm. Work in St st and stripe pat, inc 1 st each side every row 6th row 5 (6, 6) times—29 (33, 36) sts. Work even until piece measures 8 (9, 9½)"/20.5 (23, 24)cm from beg. Bind off.

FINISHING

Block pieces to measurements. Sew shoulder seams.

Neckband

With RS facing and A, pick up and k40 (42, 42) sts evenly around neck edge. Work in k1, p1 rib for 1"/2.5cm. Bind off. Place markers 4½ (5, 5½)"/11.5 (12.5, 14)cm down from shoulders on front and back. Sew sleeves between markers. Sew side and sleeve seams. Sew on buttons.

HAT

With A, cast on 28 (30) sts. Work in k1, p1 rib for 1"/2.5cm. Work in St st and stripe pat until piece measures 13"/33cm from beg. With A, work in k1, p1 rib for 1"/2.5cm. Bind off.

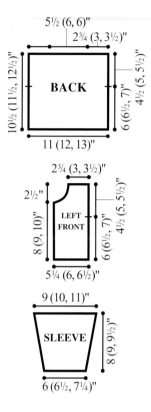

FINISHING

Fold hat in half lengthwise and sew side seams. Make two 2"/5cm pompoms, 1 with A and 1 with B and attach to top corners of hat.

MITTENS

With A, cast on 20 sts. Work in k1, p1 rib for 1½"/4cm. Work in St st and stripe pat until piece measures 4"/10cm from beg. **Next row (RS)** *K2, k2tog; rep from * to end—15 sts. Work 1 row even.
Next row (RS) *K1, k2tog; rep from * to end—10 sts. Work 1 row even.
Next row (RS) *K2tog; rep from * to end—5 sts. Cut yarn, leaving a long tail for sewing and pull through sts. Fasten off. Sew seam.

Cut three 18"/45.5cm pieces of yarn, 2 lengths in A, 1 in B, and braid. Knot ends and attach each end to inside of mitten.

POMPOM TEMPLATE

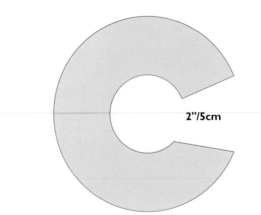

2"/5cm

■ POMPOMS

Plush pompoms make a fun finish for a kid's (or whimsical adult's) hat. Here is an easy way to construct them. When you've finished making the pompoms, simply sew to the corners of the hat.

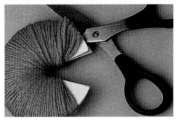

1 With two circular pieces of cardboard the width of the desired pompom, cut a center hole. Then cut a pie-shaped wedge out of the circle. Use template on previous page as a guide.

2 Hold the two circles together and wrap the yarn tightly around the cardboard. Carefully cut around the cardboard.

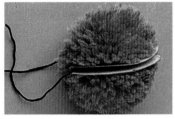

3 Tie a piece of yarn tightly between the two circles.

4 Remove the cardboard and trim the pompom.

IN THE HOOD

The perfect garment for bowing your head to the cold and digging your hands deep into your pockets, this hooded jacket, designed by Veronica Manno, is also a blast to make. The pockets are constructed using one of the most common methods, and the assembly of the hood helps you practice seaming two bound-off edges with invisible horizontal seaming.

SIZES
Instructions are written for size Small. Changes for Medium and Large are in parentheses.

KNITTED MEASUREMENTS
- Bust 34 (36, 38)"/86 (91.5, 96.5)cm
- Length 20 (21, 22)"/51 (53, 56)cm
- Upper arm 11¼ (12, 12¾)"/28.5 (30.5, 32)cm

MATERIALS
- 6 3½oz/100g balls (each approx 109yd/100m) of Rowan Yarns *Polar* (wool) in #648 blue (5)
- One pair size 11 (8mm) needles *or size to obtain gauge*
- Stitch holders
- 30"/76cm leather cord

GAUGE
12 sts and 16 rows to 4"/10cm over St st using size 11 (8mm) needles.
Take time to check gauge.

KI, PI RIB
Row I (RS) *K1, p1; rep from * to end.
Row 2 K the knit and p the purl sts.
Rep row 2 for k1, p1 rib.

K2, P2 RIB
Row I (RS) *K2, p2; rep from * to end.
Row 2 K the knit sts and p the purl sts.
Rep row 2 for k2, p2 rib.

BACK
Cast on 51 (54, 57) sts. Work in k1, p1 rib for 3 rows. Work in St st until piece measures 13"/33cm from beg.
Armhole shaping
Bind off 3 sts at beg of next 2 rows, dec 1 st each side every other row 3 times—39 (42, 45) sts. Work even until armhole measures 7 (8, 9)"/18 (20.5, 23)cm. Bind off all sts.

POCKET LININGS
(make 2)
Cast on 16 sts. Work in St st for 3"/7.5cm. Place sts on a holder.

LEFT FRONT

Cast on 25 (27, 29) sts. Work as for back until piece measures 5"/12.5cm from beg, end with a WS row.

Pocket joining

Next row (RS) Work 3 (5, 7) sts, place next 16 sts on holder for pocket opening, with k side of one pocket lining facing, k16 sts from holder, work to end. Work even until same length as back to armhole. Shape armhole at side edge (beg of RS rows) as for back—19 (21, 23) sts. Work even until armhole measures 5 (6, 7)"/12.5 (15, 18)cm, end with a RS row.

Neck shaping

Next row (WS) Bind off 5 sts (neck edge), work to end. Cont to bind off from neck edge 2 sts twice, 1 st once. Bind off rem 9 (11, 13) sts for shoulder.

RIGHT FRONT

Work to correspond to left front, reversing pocket placement as foll: **Next row (RS)** Work 6 sts, place next 16 sts on a holder for pocket opening, with k side of one pocket lining facing, k 16 sts from holder, work to end.

Reverse armhole shaping by working decs at beg of WS rows or end of RS rows, and reverse neck shaping by working decs at beg of RS rows.

SLEEVES

Cast on 24 (26, 28) sts. Work in k1, p1 rib for 3 rows. Work in St st, inc 1 st each side every 12th row 5 times—34 (36, 38) sts. Work even until piece measures 17"/43cm from beg.

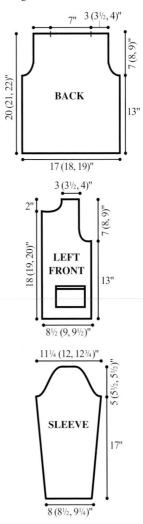

Cap shaping

Bind off 3 sts at beg of next 2 rows, dec 1 st each side every other row 8 (9, 9) times. Bind off 2 sts at beg of next 2 rows. Bind off rem 8 (8, 10) sts.

FINISHING

Block pieces to measurements. Sew shoulder seams.

Hood

Pick up 53 sts around neck edge. Work in St st for 4 rows. Mark center st.

Next row (RS) Work to 1 st before marked st, inc 1 st in next st, slip marker, inc 1 st in next st, work to end. Cont in this way to inc 1 st each side of center st every 4th row 3 times more—61 sts. Work even until hood measures 10½"/26.5cm.

Next row (RS) Work to 2 sts before marked st, k2tog, slip marker, k2tog, work to end. Cont to dec 1 st each side of center st every other row 8 times more—43 sts. Bind off. Fold in half and sew seam.

Pocket edging

Pick up sts from pocket holders and work 3 rows in k2, p2 rib. Bind off. Sew side of pocket edging to front pockets.

Set in sleeves. Sew side and sleeve seams.

Crochet edging

With RS facing and crochet hook, work 1 row of reverse sc (see page 77) around front and hood edges. Tie leather cord at front edge as shown in photo.

JOINING POCKET LINING

With the right side of the lining facing the wrong side of the piece, work the stitches of the lining from the holder, then work to the end of the row.

HOLD EVERYTHING

One of the best ways to show off your talents is with an accessory you can take everywhere. Sure to become one of your favorites, this felted bag, designed by Gretchen Strahle, boasts a rare combination of style, versatility and durability.

KNITTED MEASUREMENTS
Approx 9½" x 8"/24 x 20.5cm
(after felting)

MATERIALS
▥ 2 2oz/57g skeins (each approx 140yd/ 128m) of Green Mountain Spinnery *Mountain Mohair* (wool/mohair) each in claret (A), rhubarb (B), day lily (C), coral bell (D) and partridge berry (E) (**4**)

▥ One pair each sizes 10½ and 13 (6.5 and 9mm) needles *or size to obtain gauge*

GAUGE
11 sts and 14 rows to 4"/10cm over St st using larger needles.
Take time to check gauge.

BAG
STRIP I
(make 2)
With larger needles and 1 strand A and B held tog, cast on 19 sts. Work in St st for

25 rows. Cut B, add 1 strand C. With 1 strand A and 1 strand C held tog, cont in St st for 25 rows. Bind off.

STRIP 2
(make 2)
Work as for strip 1, using 1 strand A and 1 strand D held tog for first 25 rows, and 1 strand A and 1 strand E held tog for 2nd 25 rows.

KNITTING WITH TWO STRANDS HELD TOGETHER

To prevent the two strands you're knitting with from tangling themselves into a hideous mess, try these tips:

1 Make sure all balls are wound into center-pull skeins (see directions for making these on page 72) before beginning. This prevents the balls from rolling around and getting all twisted.

2 Place individual skeins into fold-over sandwich baggies, configuring them so that only the working strand flows out of the bag.

FINISHING

Sew strips together as in diagram below. Sew end strips together to make tube. Turn inside out. To sew bottom of bag, with 1 strand A, sl st stripes together along B and D edges. With 1 strand A, work 1 row sc and 1 row reverse sc (see page 77) around top of bag.

HANDLES

(make 2)

With smaller needles and 2 strands A held tog, cast on 6 sts. Work in garter st for 15"/38cm. Bind off. Sew handles to top of bag (see page 88).

Foll felting instructions on page 91.

A/C	A/E	A/C	A/E
A/B	A/D	A/B	A/D

FULLING AROUND

▪ FELTING

The greatest thing about felting (also called fulling) is that it never turns out quite the same way twice, making each project completely unique. The level of felting to which you aspire is largely a matter of preference: you can make your bag smaller or larger, firmer or softer depending on how long you let it tumble around in the washing machine. Our advice? Have fun with it! You're the master of the craft here.

Before we start, you should know that while felting is not a difficult process, the choice of yarn-to-be-felted is an important one. White wool (because of the way it's processed) doesn't felt well, and nor does superwash or machine–washable wool. Make sure there are no synthetic fibers in the mix of wool you buy (e.g. 70% wool, 30% acrylic), because acrylic is actually meant to go in the washer and dryer, and no matter how long you wash it, it'll never felt. The fibers that you can combine with wool for felting are mohair and alpaca, and alpaca even felts well all by itself. When combining wool and mohair for felting, choose a yarn that has the two spun together. One mohair strand held together with one wool strand tends to complicate and lengthen the felting process.

Once you've chosen the right yarn and knitted the bag, it's time to felt! The two things that yarn needs most in order to seize up and form a nice, sturdy fabric are hot water and agitation, so set the washing machine for as sturdy a fabric and as high a temperature as possible.

Fill the washer tub about half full with water and add just a little bit (maybe ¼ cup or less) of a gentle detergent. Place the purse into a large lingerie sac, drop it in the washer, and close the lid. Let the machine run for 15-20 minutes, and then stop the cycle to check your bag. Is it small enough and/or firm enough for you? If not, stick it back in for as long as it takes until you have an emphatic YES! to both questions. Every time you check its progress, you can pull and mold the bag to be the exact shape you desire.

Don't worry if you have to wash the bag for quite some time before getting the right result; it may take your bag as long as an hour or more of twisting and turning in the big metal tub before the felting is finished. Once the purse looks perfect to your eyes, let the washing machine run the rest of its cycle so that the bag emerges well-rinsed and wrung-out. You can either air dry the damp bag or toss it in the dryer on a low setting for about 10-20 minutes.

BUILDING BLOCKS

Textures abound, this sampler baby blanket teaches you five new stitch patterns—each one simply a combination of the basic knit and purl stitches you've been using all along. Each square is made individually and sewn together at the end, making this the ideal "on-the-go" project. For placement, arrange the squares as you like or refer to our illustrated diagram. Designed by Sandi Prosser.

KNITTED MEASUREMENTS
Approx 26" x 32"/66 x 81cm

MATERIALS
▪ 1 3½oz/100g ball (each approx 215yd/195m) of Colorado Yarns *Knitaly* (wool) each in #3430 lilac (A), #3821 aqua (B), #11940 purple (C), #25257 green (D) and #1363 lt blue (E) (3)

▪ 2 balls in #41952 blue (MC)

▪ One pair size 6 (4mm) needles *or size to obtain gauge*

GAUGE
21 sts and 30 rows to 4"/10cm over St st using size 6 (4mm) needles.
Take time to check gauge.

BLANKET

SQUARE I - GARTER ST
(make 4 with MC)
Cast on 32 sts. Work in garter st (k every row) until piece measures 6"/15cm from beg. Bind off.

SQUARE 2 - SEED ST
(make 4 with A)
Seed stitch
Row I (RS) K1, *p1, k1; rep from * to end.
Rep row 1 for seed st.

Cast on 31 sts. Work in seed st until piece measures 6"/15cm from beg, end with a WS row. Bind off.

SQUARE 3 - MOSS STITCH
(make 4 with B)
Moss st
Rows I and 3 (RS) Knit.
Row 2 P1, *k1, p1; rep from * to end.
Row 4 K1, *p1, k1; rep from * to end.
Rep rows 1-4 for moss st.

Cast on 31 sts. Work in moss st until piece measures 6"/15cm from beg, end with a WS row. Bind off.

SQUARE 4 – DASH STITCH

(make 4 with C)

Dash stitch

Row I (RS) K3, *p6, k4; rep from * to last 3 sts, k3.

Row 2 and all WS rows K1, p to last st, k1.

Row 3 Knit.

Row 5 K1, p3, k4, *p6, k4; rep from * to last 4 sts, p3, k1.

Row 7 Knit.

Row 8 K1, p to last st, k1.

Rep rows 1-8 for dash st.

Cast on 32 sts. Work in dash st until piece measures 6"/15cm from beg, end with a RS row. Bind off purlwise.

SQUARE 5 – LADDER STITCH

(make 4 with D)

Ladder stitch

Rows I and 3 (RS) Knit.

Row 2 K2, *p4, k2; rep from * to end.

Row 4 P2, *p1, k2, p3; rep from * to end.

Rep rows 1-4 for ladder st.

Cast on 32 sts. Work in ladder st until piece measures 6"/15cm from beg, end with a WS row. Bind off.

SQUARE 6 – REVERSE ST ST CHEVRON

(make 4 with E)

Reverse St st chevron

Row I (RS) K1, p1, *k5, p1; rep from * to last st, k1.

Row 2 K3, *p3 k3; rep from * to end.

Row 3 K2, *p2, k1; rep from * to last st, k1.

Row 4 K1, p2, *k3, p3; rep from * to last 6 sts, k3, p2, k1.

Row 5 K4, p1, *k5, p1; rep from * to last 4 sts, k4.

Row 6 K1, p to last st, k1.

Rep rows 1-6 for reverse St st chevron.
Cast on 33 sts. Work in reverse St st chevron until piece measures 6"/15cm from beg, end with a WS row. Bind off.

FINISHING
Sew squares together as illustrated in placement diagram.
Top and bottom edgings
With MC, pick up and k104 sts evenly along top of blanket. Work in garter st for 6 rows. Bind off. Work in same way along bottom edge.
Side edgings
With MC, pick up and k158 sts evenly along side of blanket. Work as for top and bottom edgings.

PLACEMENT DIAGRAM

2	4	3	5
5	6	2	1
3	1	5	4
4	2	6	3
6	5	1	2
1	3	4	6

WORDS OF WISDOM

QUICK FIX

■ CORRECTING MISTAKES

You may think that by having to turn to this section you're admitting defeat, but that's incredibly far from the truth. Good knitters make mistakes. Excellent knitters make mistakes. Even expert knitters make mistakes every now and then. And as long as you know how to fix your errors, it's no big deal. Here we've outlined (and explained how to fix) some of the most common errors that plague beginners as well as veterans in the knitting world.

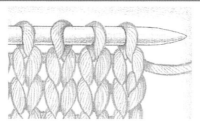

Knit Side
A twisted or backward stitch is created either by wrapping the yarn incorrectly on the previous row or by dropping a stitch and returning it to the needle backward.

To correct the backward knit stitch, knit it through the back loop.

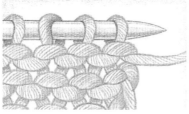

Purl Side
A backward purl stitch looks different from a regular purl stitch in that the back loop is nearer to the tip of the needle than the front loop.

To correct the backward purl stitch, purl it through the back loop.

Knit Side

1 This method is used when a knit stitch has dropped only one row. Work to where the stitch was dropped. Be sure that the loose strand is behind the dropped stitch.

2 Insert the right needle from front to back into the dropped stitch and under the loose horizontal strand behind.

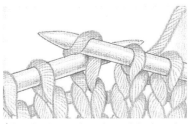

3 Insert the left needle from the back into the dropped stitch on the right needle, and pull this stitch over the loose strand.

4 Transfer this newly made stitch back to the left needle by inserting the left needle from front to back into the stitch and slipping it off the right needle.

Purl Side

I This method is used when a purl stitch has been dropped only one row. Work to the dropped purl stitch. Be sure that the loose horizontal strand is in front of the dropped stitch.

2 Insert the right needle from back to front into the dropped stitch, and then under the loose horizontal strand.

3 With the left needle, lift the dropped stitch over the horizontal strand and off the right needle.

4 Transfer the newly made purl stitch back to the left needle by inserting the left needle from front to back into the stitch and slipping it off the right needle.

Knit Side

A running stitch is one that has dropped more than one row. It is easiest to pick it up with a crochet hook. For a knit stitch, be sure the loose horizontal strands are in back of the dropped stitch.

Insert the hook into the stitch from front to back. Catch the first horizontal strand and pull it through. Continue up until you have worked all the strands. Place the newest stitch on the left needle, making sure it is not backward.

Purl Side

Before picking up a dropped purl stitch several rows below, be sure that the loose horizontal strands are in front of the stitch.

Insert the hook into the stitch from back to front. Pull the loose strand through the stitch. Continue up until you have worked all the strands. Place the newest stitch on the left needle, making sure it is not backward.

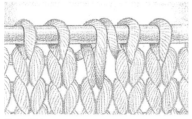

Knit Side

An incomplete knit or purl stitch is one where the yarn is wrapped around the needle but not pulled through the stitch. The illustration above shows an incomplete stitch from the previous purl row.

Work to the incomplete stitch. Insert the right needle from back to front into the stitch on the left needle and pull it over the strand and off the needle.

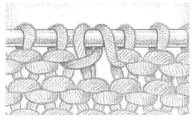

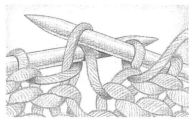

Purl Side

This illustration shows an incomplete stitch from the previous knit row.

Insert the right needle into the stitch on the left needle and pull it over the strand and off the needle.

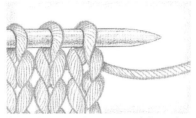

Knit Side

If you bring the yarn back over the top of the needle at the beginning of the knit row, the first stitch will have two loops instead of one, as shown.

To avoid creating this extra stitch, keep the yarn under the needle when taking it to the back to knit the first stitch.

Purl Side

At the beginning of a purl row, if the yarn is at the back, and then brought to the front under the needle, the first stitch will have two loops instead of one, as shown.

To avoid making these two loops, the yarn should be at the front before you purl the first stitch.

LONG LIVE YOUR KNITS!

CARING FOR YOUR CREATIONS

Now that you've spent all this time, energy, and money crafting your handmade masterpieces, you should know how to take care of them so that they last and last. Follow these guidelines to ensure a long, happy, healthy lives for your beautiful knits.

Reading the Ball Band

You know that little piece of paper wrapped around a brand new ball or hank of yarn? That's the ball band, and it's your friend. This label contains crucial information about how to care for the yarn when it's made up into a garment, so always start there when contemplating giving your scarf, hat, sweater or blanket a little TLC.

If at first you look at the ball band and just feel confused, you're not alone. Here are some explanations of what you might find on that all-important piece of paper that will help you care for your knitted fabric.

1 Fiber content
2 Methods of cleaning: dry-clean only, hand or machine wash, plus suggested water temperatures.
3 Bleaching (permitted or not)
4 Pressing (suggested temperatures)
5 Dry cleaning (which solutions can be used to clean the yarn).

Cleaning

The most important thing to remember when washing a sweater is this: If the conditions are too hot, too agitating or too harsh, the sweater will shrink. It's as simple as that. To prevent a sweater that took you two months to make from turning into a piece of fashionable doll clothing, follow these instructions.

Turn the garment inside out and close any buttons (to help keep things in shape). Fill a basin with cool water (the kitchen sink works well for this) and a mild soap (not detergent—too harsh). Let the sweater soak for fifteen to twenty minutes, gently swishing it around in the suds. Don't pull or twist the sweater—the less it's handled the better. Rinse in cool water three to four times until there are no more traces of soap, then squeeze out the sweater on the side of the sink until it's no longer dripping. Lay it flat on a terrycloth towel and gently but firmly roll the towel towards the opposite end to squeeze out even more water. When you think you've eked out as much wet stuff as you can, move onto the instructions for blocking and drying below.

Depending on the yarn used in your project, you may be able to put it in the washing machine (and maybe even the dryer!). Check the ball band for specific instructions. If the yarn you used is dry-clean only, let your dry cleaner know of the fiber content and/or recommended solvents to ensure the best possible result.

Blocking & Drying

Okay, so now you have a wet sweater that smells a little bit like wet sheep (don't worry—this will go away). Time to dry it flat and fast.

Always dry sweaters flat on a terrycloth towel or sweater-drying rack. Set away from direct heat and sunlight which can shrink, fade or discolor the sweater and make the fibers brittle. Reshape the sweater with your hands, pushing ribs into place and molding the neckline, hem and cuffs (just like you did for initial blocking). If necessary, pin the garment to its original measurements using rust-proof or plastic T-pins. If you take care when drying your sweater, you won't have to steam or re-block it at all.

"Why do I have to dry it fast?" you ask. Without getting too graphic, we have one word: mildew. "Gross! The last thing I want is a mildewed sweater," you reply. We totally agree on that one. In order to dry your sweater fast, follow these simple tips:

1 Change terrycloth towels under the garment often.

2 Consider investing in a sweater dryer, a handy little device that is made of mesh and can be propped over a bathtub or sink.

3 Turn the sweater over as often as necessary to allow both sides to dry.

4 Dry your sweater in a warm (but not hot or sunlit) place. Sweaters dry more slowly when the air around them is also cold and damp.

Final tips

1 Mending should always be done before cleaning.

2 Spot clean your garment between wearings so stains won't set.

3 Save a few yards of yarn from your project, wind into a figure-8 and attach securely to an inside seam. It will "age" with the sweater and ensure a color match if you should need to make repairs later.

4 Never hang handmade sweaters on a hanger, hook or the back of chair—this will pull the garment out of shape.

5 Always fold your sweaters, stack them in a staggered fashion and store the stack in a cool, dry place. Tuck a few cedar blocks in between sweaters to repel moths.

NOTES

NOTES

NOTES

RESOURCES

Write to the yarn companies listed below for purchasing and mail-order information.

BERROCO, INC.
P.O. Box 367
Uxbridge, MA 01569

BROWN SHEEP CO.
100662 County Road 16
Mitchell, NE 69357

CLASSIC ELITE YARNS
300A Jackson Street
Lowell, MA 01852

COLINETTE YARNS
distributed by
Unique Kolours

COLORADO YARNS
P.O. Box 217
Colorado Springs, CO 80903

DEBBIE BLISS YARNS
distributed by
Knitting Fever, Inc.

FILATURA DI CROSA
distributed by
Tahki•Stacy Charles, Inc.

GREEN MOUNTAIN SPINNERY
P.O. Box 568
Puntney, VT 05346

JCA
35 Scales Lane
Townsend, MA 01469

KARABELLA YARNS, INC.
1201 Broadway, Suite 311
New York, NY 10001

KNITTING FEVER, INC.
P. O. Box 502
Roosevelt, NY 11575

LANG YARNS
distributed by
Berroco, Inc.

LION BRAND YARN CO.
34 West 15th Street
New York, NY 10011

MOKUBA
55 West 39th Street
New York, NY 10018

MUENCH YARNS
285 Bel Marin Keys Blvd,
Unit J
Novato, CA 94949

NATURWOLLE
distributed
Muench Yarns

ROWAN YARNS
4 Townsend West, Suite 8
Nashua, NH 03063

TAHKI YARNS
distributed by
Tahki•Stacy Charles, Inc.

TAHKI•STACY CHARLES, INC.
8000 Cooper Ave.
Glendale, NY 11385

UNIQUE KOLOURS
1428 Oak Lane
Downingtown, PA 199335

*Write to US resources for
mail-order availability
of yarns not listed.*

BERROCO, INC.
distributed by
S. R. Kertzer, Ltd.

CLASSIC ELITE YARNS
distributed by
S. R. Kertzer, Ltd.

DIAMOND YARN
9697 St. Laurent
Montreal, PQ H3L 2N1
and
155 Martin Ross, Unit 3
Toronto, ON M3J 2L9

LES FILS MUENCH
5640 Rue Valcourt
Brossard, PQ J4W 1C5

MOKUBA
577 Queen St. West
Toronto, ON M5V 2B6

ROWAN
distributed by
Diamond Yarn

*Not all yarns used in this
book are available in
the UK. For yarns not
available, make a
comparable substitute or
contact the US manufacturer
for purchasing and
mail-order information.*

COLINETTE YARNS
Units 2-5
Banwy Workshops
Llanfair Caereinion
Powys SY21 0SG
Tel: 01938-810128

ROWAN YARNS
Green Lane Mill
Holmfirth
West Yorks HD7 1RW
Tel: 01484-681881

SILKSTONE
12 Market Place
Cockermouth
Cumbria CA13 9NQ
Tel: 01900-821052

**THOMAS RAMSDEN
GROUP**
Netherfield Road
Guiseley
West Yorks LS20 9PD
Tel: 01943-872264

VOGUE KNITTING BEGINNER BASICS

Editorial Director
TRISHA MALCOLM

Yarn Editor
VERONICA MANNO

Art Director
CHI LING MOY

Stylist
LAURA MAFFEO

Executive Editor
CARLA S. SCOTT

Photography
**JACK DEUTSCH STUDIOS
QUE-NET STUDIOS**

Book Editor
GRETCHEN STRAHLE

Copy Editor
MICHELLE LO

Book Publishing Coordinator
CARA BECKERICH

Patterns Editor
KAREN GREENWALD

Production Manager
DAVID JOINNIDES

Knitting Editor
JEAN GUIRGUIS

President, Sixth&Spring Books
ART JOINNIDES